When Good Jobs Go Bad

When Good Jobs Go Bad

Globalization, De-unionization, and Declining Job Quality in the North American Auto Industry

JEFFREY S. ROTHSTEIN

Rutgers University Press

New Brunswick, New Jersey, and London

Library of Congress Cataloging-in-Publication Data
Rothstein, Jeffrey S.
When good jobs go bad : globalization, de-unionization, and declining job quality in the
North American auto industry / Jeffrey S. Rothstein.
pages cm
Includes bibliographical references and index.
ISBN 978–0–8135–7606–0 (hardcover : alk. paper)—ISBN 978–0–8135–7605–3
(pbk. : alk. paper)—ISBN 978–0–8135–7607–7 (e-book (epub))—ISBN
978–0–8135–7608–4 (e-book (web pdf))
1. Automobile industry and trade—North America—Management. 2. Automobile industry
workers—North America. 3. Industrial relations—North America. 4. Globalization—
Economic aspects. I. Title.
HD9710.N572R67 2016
338.7'629222097—dc23   2015021890

A British Cataloging-in-Publication record for this book is available from the British Library.

Visit our website: http://rutgerspress.rutgers.edu

Manufactured in the United States of America

For Anne, Elliot, and Simon

Contents

Acknowledgments

The seeds of this book were planted in 1993. A recent college graduate, I was working for a labor union on the unsuccessful campaign to defeat the North American Free Trade Agreement (NAFTA). During a strategy session, I pointed out that the number of jobs we were arguing would be lost under NAFTA was small relative to the size of the U.S. economy. Instead, I suggested that we should be discussing the impact NAFTA might have on work itself in North America. "But Jeff," I was told, "we can't fit that on a bumper sticker."

It has been a long journey from then to the publication of this book. Fortunately, I have had many people guide and support me along the way. At the University of Wisconsin–Madison, Jonathan Zeitlin saw in me a scholar. Jonathan made sure I did not get lost in the rubble of the crumbling Industrial Relations Research Institute (1947–2003) and remained a great source of feedback and advice after I moved on get my PhD in sociology. Through Jonathan, I met Dave Trubek, with whom I worked, laughed, and argued for most of graduate school while coordinating his various forays into issues of labor in the global economy. Gay Seidman encouraged me to pursue sociology, took me under her wing, guided this research, and has been an ongoing source of feedback. For all the mentoring, I'm even more grateful for the friendship we share.

The Sociology Department proved a rich intellectual and social environment. Jane Collins, Erik Olin Wright, Joel Rogers, and Bob Freeland were among the many members of the faculty who taught me to think sociologically and influenced the analysis in this book. I also owe much to the friendships I made in graduate school and continue to enjoy. Josh Whitford, Matt Vidal, Steve McKay, Sarah Swider, Sasha Gorman, Roland Zullo, Susie Mannon, and Nancy Plankey-Videla have all been sources of critique, analysis, support, and good humor.

Research for this book included fieldwork in three different sites over roughly five years. It would not have possible without various forms of funding from the MacArthur Foundation Global Studies Fellowship at the University of Wisconsin, the Social Science Research Council's International Pre-Dissertation Fellowship Program, as well as its Program on the Corporation as a Social Institution. At the University of Wisconsin, additional funding came from the Center for World Affairs and the Global Economy, the Center for International Business Education and Research, and Latin American, Caribbean & Iberian Studies.

This book would not have been possible without the participation of all the individuals I interviewed and got to know. I am grateful to GM's managers and the union officials at each site, who took the time to answer my questions. Most important, the men and women working on GM's assembly lines in Janesville, Arlington, and Silao willingly shared their experiences, hopes, dreams, and frustrations with me. Their stories proved instrumental in crafting the book's argument.

Several people helped facilitate my fieldwork. In Janesville, Jim and Mary Zachow made me feel welcome in their bar, as did their regular clientele. Zachow's became a convenient place to meet people and touch base with my regular contacts. Mike DuPré at the *Janesville Gazette* shared with me his historical knowledge of the Janesville plant and arranged my access to the *Gazette*'s file cabinet of newspaper clippings about the plant dating back almost ninety years.

Though Janesville is a short drive from where I was living in Madison, Wisconsin, this research began in Mexico, where I was in far less familiar territory. Fortunately, Jorge Carrillo invited me down to El Colegio de la Frontera Norte and helped me get started. Jorge put me in touch with Huberto Juárez Núñez, who sent me to Silao and made the all-important introduction to the union officials at SITIMM. As a result, they embraced the research. I'm not quite sure what would have become of this research without their help, or without the advice of Graciela Bensusán.

In the course of writing this book, GM's fortunes changed, and so did my analysis. Along the way, I benefited from a variety of feedback. Dan

Clawson's comments on an early draft helped me frame the argument. Gay Seidman, Nancy Plankey Videla, and an anonymous reviewer helped me further refine and structure it. Joel Stillerman, Laurel Westbrook, and Rachel Campbell, all friends and colleagues at Grand Valley State University, helped me hone the introduction and conclusion.

I am most thankful to my wife and partner, Anne, and my two sons, Elliot and Simon. This project has been a part of their lives as long as I have. Anne and I met shortly before research for this project began. She put up with my physical absences to conduct fieldwork in Mexico and Texas, as well as my mental wanderings as analysis pervaded daily life. Over the years, Anne has read, commented on, and argued with me over a lot of my writing. This book is far better for her enthusiasm, theoretical interventions, and willingness to critique and challenge my work even when I did not want to hear it. Elliot and Simon have never known a time I was not working on this project. I thank them for their patience and understanding, or at least for just putting up with all the time I spent squirreled away in my office, simultaneously home but unavailable. But I am also grateful for all the times they gave me the perfect excuse to take a break from writing, have some fun, and do something really important.

When Good Jobs Go Bad

1

Introduction

**Three Auto Plants in
the Global Economy**

In the early 2000s, sport utility vehicles (SUVs) were among the most popular and profitable cars in the United States, and the bigger they were the better. To keep pace with demand, General Motors (GM) assembled its array of full-sized SUVs at three different North American factories, one in Mexico and two in the United States. In each plant, the chassis would pass down one assembly line where the engine, transmission, axles and tires—most of the parts of a car that actually make it go—were installed. The body of the car, where passengers sit, was welded together in a body shop before moving on to the paint department. The painted bodies then made their way through final assembly, gaining seats, dashboards, carpets, trim, and all the components we expect to find in a new car. Eventually, each chassis was "married" to a body and the final parts added. While each small truck traveled from one end of the plant to the other as it took shape, each of the several thousand assembly-line workers at each plant stayed in one place, performing a specific set of tasks over and over. At the end of the line, one of those workers would drive a shiny new GMC Yukon, Cadillac

Escalade, or Chevy Suburban, Tahoe, or Avalanche off the assembly line and out the door to await shipping.

In Mexico, Héctor[1] woke early in the morning and slipped into his GM uniform—a pair of black denim jeans, work boots, and a blue polo shirt with GM's logo embroidered over the left breast. After a bite to eat and a cup of coffee, he walked to the nearby bus stop to catch the GM employee bus that transported him from his home in Irapuato to the auto plant a little over twenty miles away in Silao, a small city in the central state of Guanajuato. Héctor returned home about twelve hours later, after a full day of work that mostly required him to follow a carefully choreographed routine to repeatedly place a small series of parts on a partially built vehicle passing before him.

Héctor was lucky. GM's plant in Silao offered among the best blue-collar jobs in the region. Héctor had been working there since shortly after the factory opened in 1994. In his early thirties nearly a decade later, Héctor's pay of U.S. $175 for a five-day, forty-eight-hour work week was more than he could earn elsewhere, and steady enough to qualify him for a government-sponsored, low-interest mortgage with which he purchased the small house he shared with his wife and two boys. Still, Héctor envisioned more. He dreamed of sending his children to college, and thought GM could afford to help him do so, if the automaker would pay him even a fraction of what his counterparts earned in the United States.

More than two thousand miles north, in Janesville, Wisconsin, Linda likewise awoke early and dressed, typically in blue jeans, a comfortable T-shirt she didn't mind getting dirty, and a pair of running sneakers that cushioned her feet during the long day ahead. She grabbed a bite to eat before hopping in her car for the short drive down to the plant. Linda trusted her teenage daughter to get herself up and off to school. They would see each other later, after Linda's shift. Linda worked ten-hour days, Monday through Thursday, and on Friday if GM needed the extra production. Working Friday was a mixed blessing. It paid time-and-a-half, but meant another whole shift doing the monotonous and repetitive work she hated. Like many of her coworkers, Linda felt trapped by the assembly line and the income it provided. She earned over $25 an hour, which, like Héctor in Mexico, made her among the highest paid unskilled blue-collar workers in the region and the country. She had landed the job in 1996, ostensibly on a temporary basis. But seventeen years later, and now a single mom in her forties, Linda worried that GM's Janesville plant, the automaker's oldest assembly facility, would close before she got the thirty years' employment she needed to collect a full pension. Then she would be faced with a dilemma many at GM have faced: whether or not to uproot her daughter and move away from family and friends to stay employed by the company.

Such a move might take Linda to Arlington, Texas, where John had relocated more than a decade earlier. Originally from Flint, Michigan, John graduated from high school there and followed his father into the sprawling complex known as Buick City. As GM shuttered the facility, John became one of a growing number of so-called GM Gypsies[2] who exercised their right under the labor contract to maintain their employment with the automaker by transferring to a different location. After a couple such moves, John, his wife, and son wound up in Arlington. Like Linda, John woke early and drove himself to the plant for a long day on the assembly line, repeatedly performing a small series of tasks. He continued to do so to support his family, understanding that a man with his education was lucky to have such an income. Well into his fifties, with almost thirty years working on assembly lines, John looked forward to retirement. He was proud to be among the many in his family to have made a career in the auto industry. But times had changed and John expected his son to go to college.

While at different stages of their careers, and at three different factories in two different countries, these three workers echoed a refrain I heard time and again over the course of this research. On the one hand, all three recognized they had among the best blue-collar jobs available— good enough to warrant moving cross-country. On the other hand, these jobs no longer seemed to offer what they once had. For Linda and John the work itself had become more demanding as GM sought to keep them in constant motion by standardizing work routines. GM's benchmark was to keep each worker moving for fifty-five seconds of each minute. For Héctor, there was a sense that his job would not fulfill the middle-class aspirations so often attached to work in the auto industry. Something had changed. And whether autoworkers were taking advantage of a new opportunity in Silao or were struggling to maintain their standard of living in Janesville and Arlington, almost all the workers attributed their situation, at least in part, to the globalization of the economy.

Three Cases of Globalization

Concerns for labor in the global economy typically focus more on sweatshops than on auto plants. A fire in a Chinese factory making toys for export to the United States or a building collapse in Bangladesh where name-brand garments are sewn makes headlines that draw a direct link between consumers in the West and exploited workers halfway around the world. Retailers and branded marketers scramble to control the damage to their image, pointing out they do not own and operate the factories, and assuring the public of their commitment to fair pay and decent working conditions. They promise to redouble their efforts to vet contractors to ensure such tragedies never happen again. Scholars, too, have shined a spotlight on sweatshops to analyze and understand why they seem such a persistent problem and what we might do about them. Supply chains have been traced, enhancing our understanding of the ways global markets place downward pressure on wages and working conditions. Likewise, the efforts of activists to raise wages and working conditions, often through consumer-based campaigns to hold retailers accountable, have been studied and critiqued for their effectiveness.[3]

Yet the impact of globalization on work extends far beyond the sweatshop. In fact, it can be argued that almost all workers are affected in one way or another by the opening and integration of national economies, the expansion of trade, and the ensuing economic restructuring that takes place. Not all workers will be subject to overt exploitation. But for many, the nature of their work, the availability of jobs in their industry, and the wages and benefits they receive will be impacted by the globalization of the economy. So just as understanding the reasons for the persistence of sweatshops offers insights into the worst consequences of globalization, teasing out the dynamics by which other types of employment are shaped by globalization furthers our understanding of the global economy.

How has globalization affected auto work? What dynamics of globalization are responsible? And what can the experience of autoworkers in the global economy tell us about labor in the global economy more broadly? This book explores the effect of globalization on North American autoworkers like Héctor, Linda, and John through a comparison of the organization of work and labor relations at the three GM assembly plants where they worked, and by linking their conditions of employment to the broader dynamics of economic globalization. The analysis demonstrates that the globalization of the North American auto industry has compromised job quality in the industry. The pace of work has intensified even as pay and benefits have dropped. Yet North American autoworkers have what remain among the best blue-collar jobs the global economy has to offer. If studies of sweatshops expose just how low unregulated labor conditions can be driven by global competition, this study of the auto industry shows that the negative impact of globalization on workers is much broader. Even the "good jobs" are getting worse.

At first blush, the plants in this study appear to be on different trajectories in the global economy. Héctor's workplace in Silao was a "greenfield site," a brand-new, state-of-the-art facility, built in a previously unindustrialized area. A direct consequence of the globalization of the North American auto industry, the factory and its workforce appeared to have a bright future. By contrast, Linda's workplace in Janesville, Wisconsin, was GM's oldest operating facility, dating to 1919. Its days were seen as numbered by management and labor alike; it closed at the end of 2008 when demand for SUVs declined and GM's bankruptcy hit. The third facility, where John worked, in Arlington, Texas, was midway between the other two, both geographically and in terms of age. Its future was neither as secure as Silao's nor as imperiled as Janesville's. Yet, in spite of their different fortunes in the global economy, the factories bore striking similarities in the manner they assembled GM's full-sized SUVs. At each facility, the automaker's Global Manufacturing System (GMS) required assembly-line work to be organized into carefully choreographed routines. This similarity reveals a common underlying trajectory of declining job quality within the auto industry, even among plants with such different histories and divergent futures.

Silao—Globalization as Opportunity

Opened in 1994 on the outskirts of Silao, a small city of sixty thousand residents located in an agricultural region roughly 225 miles northwest of Mexico City, the first plant in this study was quintessentially greenfield. Lured by state policymakers determined to bring economic development and jobs to a region previously known mostly for the quality of its strawberries, the arrival of GM and other factories that followed transformed the area in and around Silao into the industrial and export center of the state of

Guanajuato. Some of the other new manufacturers were suppliers to GM that the automaker needed nearby. Others, such as Case and Weyerhauser, were taking advantage of the attractive business environment, upgraded highways, and new international airport, which state policymakers had promised GM in order to woo the automaker.

At its inception, the Silao factory assembled small pickup trucks for the Mexican market. However, the facility was built with the U.S. market in mind. As full employment and manufacturing capacity was reached, production shifted to the assembly of SUVs for export to the United States. By 2003, when my research at the plant began, a combination of 820 Chevy Suburbans, Chevy Avalanches, and Cadillac Escalade EXTs, among the largest and most profitable of the fifteen models of SUVs GM offered, rolled off the assembly line each day. Ninety percent of the vehicles were loaded onto trains destined for the United States, where the base sticker price for an Avalanche exceeded $32,000 and a fully loaded Escalade could fetch over $60,000.

In planning their operations in Silao, General Motors seized the opportunity presented by a greenfield site to start afresh—to shape an entire industrial culture and establish production, employment, and labor relations norms. Those lucky enough to land a job working at the new auto plant joined a workforce considered a blue-collar elite within the area. In fact, because the automaker offered steady work and the best pay in the region, GM received far more applications than it had positions to fill. If lucky enough to pass GM's scrutiny and gain employment, a fresh hire began a new job that one of them described as "like entering a different world."

That new world meant joining the assembly line, where line operators clad in identical uniforms worked in teams of six, rotating their jobs throughout the day. Each work station was equipped with a cord workers could pull if they were experiencing a problem. Doing so triggered the Andon system. The team's alphanumeric code flashed on overhead screens throughout the plant while the musical jingle the team was assigned began playing at their work station, so that visitors to the factory might suddenly find themselves serenaded by the theme songs to *The Simpsons* or *The Newlywed Game* television shows, or the "Hallelujah" chorus from Handel's *Messiah*. These broadcasts alerted all the team members to converge on the site of the problem to resolve the issue before it forced a stoppage of the assembly line. All manufacturing problems were to be resolved "in station," meaning that no team should ever pass a defective product to their coworkers further down the line.

During their daily half-hour meal break, workers dined in the plant's cafeteria, which offered them, their supervisors, and senior management an array of entrees, side dishes, and desserts, the nutritional value of which was posted on a table near the serving area. The centerpiece of each circular dining table was the plant's daily news bulletin, a two-sided flyer including statistics on production goals, productivity, and safety, as well as employee birthday notices, reports on the latest bonuses paid to employees for their cost-saving suggestions, and other relevant plant news. Motivational banners adorned the walls. One included a picture of a pouncing lion over a caption urging workers to help GM become "king of the automotive jungle." Another was a collage of children's smiling faces over the caption "Sí se puede, papa!"—an appropriation by GM of the rallying cry of the United Farm Workers union and other Latino social movements in the United States for the purpose of motivating assembly-line workers.

This different world of work extended beyond the plant walls, permeating nearly every aspect of the workers' lives. In hiring workers who lacked any industrial experience, GM employed many from agricultural backgrounds. The steady income workers earned offered their families previously unimagined opportunities, such as home ownership and education for their children. But the opportunities were matched by challenges. In addition to the long workday, many of GM's employees commuted on the company's buses up to an hour each way from their homes in the nearby cities of Irapuato, León, and Guanajuato. For many workers, the long hours away from home compromised their image of family life. Even the meal they ate at work represented a cultural shift, often replacing the traditional family dinner that shut many area stores from 2:00 to 4:00 in the afternoon. Such were the changes and challenges that accompanied the new opportunities in Silao.

Union officials in Silao explained that assisting workers in adapting to factory work was one of their primary functions. Workers at the plant were represented by the Union of Workers of the Metal-Mechanical, Automotive, Similar and Connected Industries of the Mexican Republic, known as SITIMM, its Spanish acronym. Even before GM hired a single employee, the automaker had chosen SITIMM to represent their workers. Upon our introduction at SITIMM's regional offices, union officials informed me that "we are not corrupt," and that I was welcome to hang out whenever I wanted and to ask them anything. SITIMM was not one of Mexico's many absentee "ghost unions" with which employers sign protection contracts to prevent workers from organizing their own unions. Rather, SITIMM was an active union, but one that espoused a philosophy of labor-management cooperation and explicitly renounced strikes and other forms of labor militancy.

Technically, SITIMM negotiated with GM over wages, but even the union's leaders acknowledged that they had little bargaining leverage with GM. Instead, the primary function of the union was to provide the support workers needed to hold on to the best blue-collar jobs in the area, a goal that paralleled GM's need to maintain low turnover rates and stability within the work teams at the heart of the production process. At times functioning almost as an extension of GM's human resources department, and with offices immediately next door, SITIMM's elected officials assisted employees in managing their incomes by helping them open bank accounts and apply for the government-subsidized home mortgages for which they qualified due to their stable employment. SITIMM also provided social support for workers with problems outside the plant by making hospital visits, organizing and paying for funerals, and even serving as ad hoc marriage counselors on occasion. Union leaders claimed to provide these services to ensure that workers' personal lives did not compromise their performance at work, so they did not lose one of the best jobs the local economy had to offer a young man with a ninth-grade education.

Janesville—Globalization as Doom

Unlike GM's model greenfield site in Silao, the two plants in the United States were well worn, with experienced workforces. The first, in Janesville, Wisconsin, employed 3,600 hourly workers, including 500 skilled tradespeople whose job it was to keep the assembly line and the plant's more than 600 robots running. The factory assembled almost 1,200 SUVs daily, a combination of Chevy Suburbans and Tahoes, and their GMC counterparts, the Yukon and Yukon Denali.

Janesville, like Silao, is a small city with a population of roughly sixty thousand people. As in Silao, GM offered workers in Janesville the best unskilled blue-collar jobs in the area, but had been doing so much longer. The plant in Janesville dated to 1919, when GM selected the site for its production of Samson Tractors, some of which were steered with reins rather than a steering wheel in order to appeal to farmers accustomed to working with horses. Over more than eight decades after GM discontinued Samson Tractor in 1923, as models and production needs changed, the plant grew from 122,000 to over 4.5 million square feet. GM's property holdings nearly tripled to 137 acres. Much of this expansion came from purchasing the homes and businesses that once stood across the street from the factory, leveling them and paving parking lots for the workers' own SUVs and pickup trucks. Almost all workers drove GM products, which they purchased at an employee discount. For those who did not, or more likely guests to the plant, a sign at the entry to the parking lot ordered all "vehicles not assembled in the U.S.A. or Canada by union workers should park in lot #11," the farthest from the plant.

The lone holdout resisting GM's accumulation of real estate was Zachow's Bar, which sold cans of beer and mixed drinks. Though on private property, Zachow's location created the appearance that GM had a bar in the middle of their parking lot. The bar's slogan, "a little bit of heaven on the gates of hell," was printed on the free matchbooks Zachow's distributed and regulars at the bar often repeated it. Local GM management and union officials preferred not to discuss Zachow's. Much like "Packer Monday," the day that the Green Bay Packers appearance on *Monday Night Football* allegedly forced a halt to production due to excessive absenteeism, from time to time Zachow's presence became a metaphor in the press for everything outdated about the Janesville plant. Rumors swirled as to how much money GM had offered to buy and destroy the bar. But Jim Zachow, whose father had opened the place, said the automaker did not offer enough to compensate him and his wife, Mary, for the brisk business they did during lunch break and shift change. Mary insisted that workers "pour more drinks inside the plant than we do out here."

Unlike in Silao, nobody wore uniforms in Janesville. Workers wore pretty much whatever they wanted, typically cut-off shorts or jeans, sneakers, and T-shirts emblazoned with the logos of their favorite sport teams or Harley Davidson motorcycles. Technically, line operators were organized into teams of workers, each with a "Team Coordinator" commonly referred to as the "TC." But these teams were mostly superficial. Team members did not rotate jobs as they did in Silao. Team coordinators did little more than replace absent workers or step in to give workers a break. In fact, many workers measured the quality of their TC based on how frequently they gave such breaks, and how quickly they responded when workers requested one.

As in Silao, workers had Andon cords at their work stations that they could pull if something went wrong. Doing so would trigger the Andon system, which was designed to promote quality by providing line operators a means of alerting their supervisors to defects in production that need to be addressed. But line operators in Janesville had learned to ignore it. Pulling the cord did not trigger team problem-solving as in Silao, it triggered managerial anxiety. Supervisors under pressure to maintain production were said to simply turn off the Andon system if activated by a worker, and to sometimes plead or shout "don't shut me down." Workers also claimed that management was unresponsive to their recommendations for improving the plant. On the other hand, one former manager indicated that instead of contributing useful suggestions, workers demanded alternative selections in the vending machines or anonymously vented profanities at their supervisors and the automaker.

So in Janesville, workers focused nearly exclusively on performing their designated routine. As in all GM's plants, in Janesville they were implementing the new GMS, which required that all jobs be meticulously choreographed. Line operators were expected to complete their standardized work in exactly the manner dictated by the company's industrial engineers, whose goal was to precisely synchronize production to keep workers in near constant motion. Workers in Janesville frequently complained that the pace of work under the GMS was excessive, with many expressing concerns about repetitive motion injuries.

The hope of most workers in Janesville was to eventually accumulate sufficient seniority to move off the assembly line to less taxing work. Workers selected their jobs through a plant-wide seniority system. As a result, just as the cars being built on the assembly line made their way around the old factory, winding in and out of the nooks and crannies of the plant's body shop, paint department, and final assembly area, work assignments could take GM's employees from one end of the plant to the other through the course of their careers. Starting with the most strenuous jobs in final assembly, workers expected to move progressively to less physically demanding work in the body shop or paint department before transferring to a job off the assembly line, so one would not have to "chase chain." This typically entailed moving into parts delivery, driving a forklift perhaps, and eventually to "unskilled maintenance," where a worker could earn over $25 an hour mopping up. One woman quipped that "this may be the only job in the world where you need thirty years' seniority before someone will let you clean the toilet."

Until a worker scored that offline job, there was near unanimity among Janesville's supervisors, union officials, and workers that keeping up the pace of production, achieving that fifty-five seconds of labor for each minute, was critical to the plant's survival. For decades, as the automaker lost market share and closed facilities, GM had been forcing assembly plants and their local unions, workers, and managerial teams to compete against one another for the product lines necessary to stay open. Due to this practice, known as "whipsawing," many in Janesville viewed GM's facilities in Silao and Arlington as the competition. Labor and management alike understood that they could not afford to give GM an excuse to close the Janesville plant and shift production elsewhere.

Given this concern for Janesville's future, the union leadership had become increasingly anxious to highlight the plant's productivity, quality workforce, and cooperative labor relations. They even expressed concerns that my research might cast the factory in a negative light and contribute to the plant's demise. Workers in Janesville were represented by United Auto Workers (UAW) Local 95, which dated to the 1937 sit-down strikes through which the UAW gained recognition from GM. Local 95's local contract embodied nearly seventy years of accumulated negotiations and outlined everything from shift hours and grievance procedures to understandings over which flags would be flown over the plant (United States, Wisconsin, UAW, and POW-MIA) and how often the trash containers in vending areas would be washed (once every two weeks). I was told that the contract used to include a provision shutting the plant for days during deer hunting season, and detailing the manner in which maintenance workers would be allocated time off while the plant was idled.

By the time I began my research, however, downtime for deer hunting and other benefits had been conceded as the focus of Local 95 turned decisively to keeping the plant open. Janesville had encountered whipsawing repeatedly since the 1980s. The plant's history of responding to whipsawing was reflected in the composition of the workforce. A portion of the workers were long-time Janesville employees, many of whom had followed parents and grandparents into the plant. Others, like Linda, were Janesville natives known as "'86ers," and not infrequently the "god-damn '86ers." They had been hired in 1986 to temporarily replace 1,200 workers who, having been convinced the Janesville plant might close, followed production of the pickup truck they built to its new home in Fort Wayne, Indiana. Instead of closing the Janesville facility as many feared, GM awarded the plant the Chevy Suburban product line after negotiating concessions in work rules from Local 95. Suddenly, the '86ers became permanent employees. After securing the Suburban assembly line, in the 1990s Janesville became a destination for a wave of GM employees whose plants had closed, often because their own local unions refused to make concessions to work rules. A final group of workers was hired in the mid-1990s, after a successful local strike to increase the workforce in order to reduce overtime, which had become mandatory as GM sought to meet the unrelenting demand for SUVs. The typical Janesville operator was in their mid-forties with over twenty years of seniority. They were a mix of men and women, most with families in the area, and most hoping they would qualify for retirement before their aging facility was shut down.

Arlington—Globalization as Threat

If globalization was associated with opportunity in Silao and imminent doom in Janesville, in Arlington it was perceived as a threat, but one that could be survived. Roughly midway between Wisconsin and Silao, the city of Arlington lies between Dallas and Fort Worth. The GM plant sits just off the highway in Arlington's dwindling industrial area, somewhat wedged between a more residential area to the south that also hosts the University of Texas–Arlington and the growing entertainment sector to the north that includes a Six Flags amusement park, the Texas Rangers baseball stadium, and the new Dallas Cowboys football stadium, which was being built at the time of this research.

Like the plant in Janesville, the factory in Arlington had survived various rounds of GM plant closures. Unlike Janesville, however, workers still move to Arlington. When I arrived in 2006, half the plant's 2,800 workers were transferees who had been in Arlington less than six years. They were typically middle-aged, with over twenty years' seniority with the company. With few other good employment options available, they had uprooted their families, some more than once, and relocated to Texas to hold on to one of the dwindling number of blue-collar manufacturing jobs paying over $25 an hour with full benefits. Many expressed resentment toward the automaker; one worker said about GM that "they lie to everyone. They lie to the workers. They lie to their own supervisors. They lie to suppliers. They lie to dealers. And they lie to customers. All they know how to do is lie."

A decade earlier, Janesville had become a popular destination for the so-called GM Gypsies, but by the year 2000 they began streaming into Arlington, so much so that local management had created a training program tailored to transferees. According to a human resources manager who had himself migrated to Texas from Michigan, "Every employee that transfers here to this facility we put through a two-week orientation program before they ever hit the shop floor . . . to orientate them to what we do here in Arlington. Other facilities have team concept, but we want to make sure that they hear and see what we do here at Arlington."

By "team concept" he was referring to the manufacturing system that predated the GMS, elements of which had been maintained in the new system. In Arlington, line operators worked in teams of seven, including the team coordinator. As in Silao and Janesville, each job was carefully scripted, and assembly-line workers were expected to repeat their tasks without deviating from the standardized routine, so that industrial engineers could fit as much work as possible into each job. Team coordinators assumed a role with somewhat greater responsibility than in Janesville, but one that was less supervisorial than in Silao. In Arlington, team coordinators led team meetings and performed some administrative duties while also filling in for workers who were off the line for some reason. Team coordinators responded when workers pulled the Andon cord and determined whether the problem needed to be addressed immediately, could be fixed later, or whether a supervisor should be alerted.

As in Janesville, workers in Arlington selected jobs according to seniority. But under the system in Arlington, available jobs were offered first to other workers already in that team. Only after all the members of the team who wanted to change their job had done so was the remaining job made available to other workers in the plant. As a result, line operators tended not to move around the plant as much as they did in Janesville. The resulting team continuity allowed the work teams in Texas to function more smoothly than they did in Wisconsin, but without the job rotation found in Silao. For workers transferring from other GM plants, however, the seniority system in Arlington required that they select among the jobs left available by everyone already working in the plant. Instead of segueing off the assembly line and toward retirement at their previous places of employment, transferees to Arlington were starting anew at what were widely considered the worst jobs in the factory.

This reality fed the resentment already felt by many transferees, some of which was directed at the local union. Workers in Arlington were represented by UAW Local 276, which, fairly or not, had a reputation throughout the UAW for acquiescing to management in order to keep their plant open. That reputation had been cemented in 1992 when Arlington won a very public whipsawing contest against GM's Willow Run assembly plant in Ypsilanti, Michigan. The Ypsilanti plant was shut down and their product line was transferred to Arlington. The publicity around events as they unfolded, and the lengths to which the local community and the union in Texas went to secure their victory over an iconic Michigan plant, turned Local 276 into the poster child for whipsawing. The claim that Local 276 was constantly "giving away the store" was a popular notion among workers and their local union officials in Janesville, in spite of their own history of making concessions to save their plant.

Unlike in Janesville, though, where the plant's days were recognized as numbered, in Arlington there was hope of longevity and a realization that keeping the plant running depended on successfully implementing the GMS. Union officials and management all claimed to work closely toward that goal. The teams and Andon system functioned as designed, and employee recommendations to management, particularly regarding ways GM could save money, were well documented and taken seriously. In fact, the Arlington plant was said to consistently lead the automaker in bonuses paid to workers for their cost-saving ideas. Unlike the facility in Janesville, labor and management believed the plant in Arlington still had long-term potential, providing that the local union continued to work cooperatively with management to implement the GMS and improve efficiency.

Auto Labor in a Global Economy

At first glance, it is tempting to see these plants as another story of capital flight in search of cheap labor made easily available in the global economy—an example of what U.S. autoworkers might view as Mexico "stealing American jobs." U.S. deindustrialization has been associated with a paucity of "good jobs" in the United States (Kalleberg 2011; Osterman and Shulman 2011). The opening of the plant in Silao, even as GM shut facilities in the United States, could be seen as a move by the automaker to take advantage of the North American Free Trade Agreement (NAFTA) to trade high-priced labor and rigid union work rules in the United States for cheaper, more malleable, and team-oriented workers in Mexico. Indeed, there is little doubt that Mexico's lower labor costs and compliant unions are attractive to manufacturers.

The other side of this analytic coin would offer a compelling picture of successful, high-road economic development in Silao. Mexico's inexpensive labor and close proximity to the U.S. market have led to concerns over labor exploitation and the growth of sweatshops, particularly along the border. By contrast, the growth of an auto industry in Silao could be seen as evidence of real economic development around a stable industrial base. Such industrial upgrading (Bair and Gereffi 2003; Gereffi 1999) could bring relatively well-paid jobs in factories engaged in technologically sophisticated manufacturing, which is sometimes seen as an indication of development itself (Carrillo and Alfredo 1998).

To pursue such an analysis, however, would be to forgo an opportunity to examine the impact of globalization on overall job quality in the North American auto industry, where labor accounts for a relatively small percentage of production costs and we do not see a mass movement of auto plants away from industrialized countries to developing regions (Silver 2003). Besides, though GM closed the Janesville plant in 2008, it had coexisted with the factory in Silao for fourteen years, and the decision to halt production in Janesville is best attributed to a combination of plunging long-term demand for SUVs and the facility's age, not a shift to cheap labor in Mexico. Instead, the plants in this study are best seen as occupying different places in a common drive toward the globalization of the North American auto industry.

Defining Globalization

What is "globalization" and what does it mean to say that the North American auto industry has undergone a process of globalization? This book is concerned with economic globalization, which I define as the increasing interconnectedness and integration of economies due to the opening of markets and the expansion of trade and investment across borders that results from international agreements (McMichael 2008; Sassen 2007).

This conception of globalization shares a common understanding of the global economy with what has elsewhere been labeled "neoliberalism" to describe the trajectory of economic policies toward unregulated free and open trade in goods and services, and the deregulation of markets in general (Clawson 2003; Webster, Lambert, and Bezuidenhout 2008). Yet the global economy is rife with "obvious violations in practice of 'free market principles'" (Evans 2008, 272). Since this is especially true of the North American auto industry, where GM and Chrysler received government bailouts and labor markets are constrained in various ways that will become apparent in this book, I avoid equating globalization with neoliberalism.

This understanding of globalization also stands in stark contrast to popular conceptions of globalization as a wave unleashed by advances in technology and communications that one can attempt to ride, but not control (Friedman 2005). While it is true that many of the workers with whom I spoke experienced globalization as an uncontrollable wave, very identifiable policies reshaped the competitive environment in which GM operated and unleashed the changes autoworkers experienced. The challenge herein is to systematically link economic globalization to those changes in the North American auto industry that have negatively affected job quality in both the United States and Mexico.

The Globalization of the North American Auto Industry—a Value Chains Approach

Understanding the impact of globalization on workers is complicated by the fact that the "global economy to a large extent materializes in national territories" (Sassen 2007, 32). Workers' experiences can often be explained through the lens of national or regional economic phenomena. Finding the link to the global economy requires "decoding particular aspects of what is still represented or experienced as national" (Sassen 2007, 19) or subnational. The North American auto industry is an important case in point. The industry has been thoroughly transformed by processes widely associated with globalization, yet remains a locus of national or subnational policy making as a source of good blue-collar jobs and local economic development. The U.S. federal government bailed out the auto industry to protect good jobs. States and counties vie to attract auto plants to create good jobs. Whether in

Wisconsin, Texas, or Guanajuato, the prospect of losing a current auto plant or attracting a new one sends politicians scurrying to offer automakers incentives. Yet, all this national and subnational activity is in response to an economic globalization that has transformed the North American auto industry, the consequences of which are reflected in the three plants in Silao, Janesville, and Arlington.

Linking the working conditions and labor relations at each of the three plants to globalization begins by explicating the transformation of the North American auto industry. This idea of studying globalization by focusing on a particular industry is at the heart of the "value chains" literature (Gereffi et al. 2001). The value chains approach calls for understanding globalization by teasing out the dynamics by which industries and their supply chains structure and restructure in response to global economic incentives. Once these value chains are understood, the roles of whole regions, nations, or specific firms and factories in the global economy may be explored through an analysis of the manner in which value chains "touch down" (Bair and Gereffi 2003, 143) in particular locations. Value chain analyses are useful, therefore, for providing insight into the manner in which industries respond to changes in the global economy and the impact these have on localities.

Value chain analyses have generally addressed labor issues only broadly, for instance by highlighting the role that demands for cost reductions from retailers in the United States play in creating sweatshop conditions among suppliers and subcontractors in low-wage countries (Gereffi 1994). Hence the emphasis the antisweatshop movement has placed on pressuring retailers to improve labor conditions among their suppliers (Featherstone 2002; Seidman 2007). But placing labor at the center of a comparative study of the globalization of a particular industry requires extending the analysis to the workplaces where the changing dynamics of the value chains shape labor relations and impact workers (Webster, Lambert, and Bezuidenhout 2008).

In the cases here, the assembly plants in Silao, Janesville, and Arlington are three locations where GM's value chain touched down within the globalized North American auto industry. While Héctor, Linda, John, and their coworkers in the United States and Mexico may only have a sense of the changes brought about by globalization, they experienced them on a day-to-day basis in their factories, where they participated in automotive assembly.

Therefore, each factory represents one outcome of a globalization of the North American auto industry that incorporates three interrelated components. First, once mutually exclusive auto industries in Mexico and the U.S.-Canada region have integrated into a single, continent-wide auto industry in which both auto parts and finished products move freely across national borders. Second, competition from outside North America, first by Japanese and then European and Korean automakers, has expanded the number of automakers selling and assembling automobiles in North America. Finally, the increased competition within the integrated North American auto industry provoked widespread industrial restructuring as well as the reorganization of work along the assembly line. The auto industry, once predicated on a mass production philosophy under which automakers sought to manufacture their automobiles from the ground up and employ workers in vast networks of parts factories as well as final assembly plants, transitioned to adopt the lean production model introduced to the continent by Toyota and other Japanese automakers. Automakers restructured, spinning off their parts divisions to focus on design, marketing, and final assembly while reorganizing work to improve efficiency. The full extent of the transformation of the North American auto industry as it globalized is described below, beginning with a brief description of the auto industry before the process of globalization began.

The Fordist Era of North American Automotive Manufacturing

Until the mid-1980s, the Mexican and U.S.-Canadian auto industries grew side by side, mutually exclusive from each other, and each largely insulated from foreign competition. Automakers operated according to the precepts of mass production, the origins of which can be found in Henry Ford's determination to market an automobile sufficiently affordable for mass consumption. Automakers employed mostly unskilled workers who performed a few specific tasks on their portion of the long, moving assembly lines that Ford pioneered.

In the United States and Canada, which integrated their auto industries through the 1965 U.S.-Canada auto pact (Holmes 1993), the economies of scale and large sales volumes required by mass production led to a winnowing of independent automakers, so that by the mid-1980s only the

Detroit Big Three (General Motors, Ford, Chrysler) remained. From the end of World War II to the late 1960s, sales of automobiles in the United States grew from roughly two million to over nine million cars per year, only 15 percent of which were imported vehicles, mostly manufactured in Europe and particularly by Volkswagen. The remainder of the market was dominated by General Motors, Ford, and Chrysler, which claimed roughly 45, 25, and 15 percent of total sales respectively (Rubenstein 1992).

In Mexico, automobile production began in 1926 with the opening of a Ford plant in Mexico City, and continued for over thirty years as an industry limited to the assembly of vehicles from parts imported from the United States (Bennett and Sharpe 1985; Middlebrook 1989; Roxborough 1984). It was not until 1962, and the initiation of the Mexican government's import substitution industrialization (ISI) economic development strategy, that the industry expanded. At that time, policymakers targeted the auto industry for growth with incentives and state investment, while shielding automakers from international competition through high tariffs and other import controls. Under the ISI policies intended to nurture the automobile industry toward eventual international competitiveness, and through which domestic manufacturers had sole access to Mexican consumers, automobile production grew from a little over 31,000 cars in 1960 to over 280,000 units in 1979 (Roxborough 1984). Production was centralized in the country's industrial heartland in and around Mexico City. Of the seven automakers, five were wholly owned subsidiaries of foreign corporations: GM, Ford, Chrysler, Nissan, and Volkswagen. The other two included Mexican capital. Vehículos Automotores Mexicanos was a joint venture, 40 percent of which was owned by American Motors. Diesel Nacional was a state-owned enterprise building cars under license to the French automaker Renault (Bennett and Sharpe 1985).

With the two automotive sectors in the U.S.-Canada and Mexico isolated from one another, automakers established vast supplier networks on each side of the border dividing the United States and Mexico. As mass production emerged from craft production in the northern part of the continent in the early twentieth century, there was no auto parts industry, and since transportation systems made reliable delivery a challenge, the automakers had to produce nearly all their own parts. This necessity developed into an organizational strategy of vertical integration, whereby automakers sought the capacity to build cars from the ground up by establishing new parts factories themselves or acquiring those of other companies.

General Motors pursued this strategy most aggressively, while Chrysler depended more on outside contractors (Kwon 2003; Womack, Jones, and Roos 1990).

On the Mexican side of the border, the automakers also developed extensive vertically integrated companies. Bound by government policies requiring 60 percent domestic content in all vehicles, and faced with a dearth of reliable independent suppliers, automakers developed their own supply chains out of necessity (Bueno 1998). For GM, Ford, and Chrysler, this meant operating parallel supply chains for each of their U.S.-Canadian and Mexican operations.

These parallel industries were maintained into the 1980s, at which time policies encouraging economic integration and increased trade began the process of integrating the two distinct and insular auto industries into a single North American auto industry. With the implementation of NAFTA, the borders became open to trade in almost all goods, including autos and auto parts. Over the same period, encouraged by the opening of markets, automakers from Asia and Europe began selling and assembling autos in the United States. As a consequence, Japanese-style lean production spread, creating a competitive imperative for automakers to restructure their firms and workplaces. Over a mere twenty-year span, automotive value chains restructured and integrated throughout the continent, forever changing the manner in which they touch down in different locations. Given the countries' different starting points, they took different paths toward an integrated North American auto industry.

From ISI to Globalization: The Integration of Mexico into the North American Auto Industry

The ISI strategies pursued in Mexico beginning in the 1950s required large investments by the Mexican government, funded by foreign debt and oil revenue. That mounting debt and a drop in the price of oil created an economic crisis in 1982 that forced the government to accede to the demands of international creditors, particularly those in the United States, and abandon ISI development policies. In very short order, the government reversed course by adopting export oriented industrialization (EOI) policies to grow the economy by promoting exports rather than by protecting the domestic market. EOI strategies were followed by increasingly neoliberal economic policies that promoted increased trade and an embrace of the global economy, but eschewed efforts to steer economic outcomes as ISI and EOI policies did. With Mexico's 1986 adoption of the General Agreement on Tariffs and Trade (GATT) and its successor, the World Trade Organization (WTO), and in signing NAFTA in 1993, the country quickly moved from isolationist economic policies to a full embrace of the global economy.

At each stage of this progression from ISI to EOI, policies were implemented to promote the development of the auto industry. Under ISI, the government had issued decrees regulating the auto industry, and this continued as the country sought to promote exports. The 1977 auto decree introduced the first hints of an opening of the border by allowing automakers to import and export products as long as they maintained an even balance of trade. The 1983 auto decree came in the wake of Mexico's default on its debt and the sharp devaluation of the peso that decimated the Mexican middle class and, consequently, domestic demand for automobiles. To save the industry by promoting exports, the government's decree limited all automakers to production of one make, or brand, of car, and five models, unless over 50 percent of any additional production would be exported. Both the 1977 and 1983 decrees continued to protect the domestic market by maintaining the 60 percent domestic content requirement for vehicles sold in Mexico. Yet the regulations simultaneously encouraged the automakers to produce cars and auto parts specifically for export to the United States (Bennett and Sharpe 1985).

The last auto decree, issued in 1989, moved Mexico's auto industry further along the road to integration with the rest of North America and began rolling back regulations designed to guide industrialization in favor of policies promoting a more laissez-faire approach. Specifically, the 1989 decree reduced the domestic content requirement for cars assembled and sold in Mexico to 36 percent and, for the first time, allowed automakers to supplement their Mexican manufactured offerings with imports. A few years later, NAFTA laid out a roadmap for complete integration of the North American auto industry. The 2.5 percent tariffs the United States charged on cars imported from Mexico, as well as the slightly higher tariffs on parts, were eliminated immediately, while the 25 percent duty on light trucks was cut to 10 percent and then phased out by 1998. Likewise, Mexican duties were phased out over five years for automobiles and ten years for parts, a schedule that Mexico eventually accelerated unilaterally (Doh 1998; Holmes 1993; Pries 2000; Ramirez de la O 1998).

The shifts in policy from ISI to EOI to NAFTA led to new investments in factories that changed the face of Mexican auto production both in terms of the products being made and the location of that production. As the automakers refocused Mexican production for export to the United States, Mexican auto plants migrated north, away from Mexico's traditional industrial heartland. In the first half of the 1980s, GM, Chrysler, and Ford all opened plants in northern Mexico (Micheli 1994). These new plants had a near immediate impact on trade. From 1982 to 1989, Mexican exports of engines and finished vehicles to the United States multiplied by a factor of four and nine, respectively (Shaiken 1990). In 1982, Mexico exported a total of 13,749 vehicles, all but 54 of which were Volkswagens. By 1990, this number had increased to a quarter million, with the Detroit automakers accounting for almost 75 percent. A similar increase can be seen in engine production for export. Chrysler and GM were each exporting about 135,000 engines from Mexico to the United States by 1982. Chrysler doubled this amount by 1986, and GM quadrupled their total by 1988. Ford, which exported one thousand engines in 1982, increased this to 275,000 by 1987 (Micheli 1994). By 2010, the United States was importing over 1.25 million automobiles from Mexico annually, for an 11 percent market share. Mexico's exports of autos, their components, and parts exceeded $45 billion (*Wall Street Journal*, February 9, 2011).

The Rise of "Foreign" Automakers in the United States and the Spread of "Transplant" Factories

As the North American auto industry was integrating, competition in the auto industry was heating up. The oil crises of the 1970s sent gasoline prices soaring, creating an instant demand in the United States for the smaller, more fuel-efficient cars produced by Japanese automakers, which had saturated their own domestic market and were looking to export to the United States (Kenney and Florida 1993). From 1972 to 1980, auto imports grew from 15 to 27 percent of the U.S. market, with Japanese automakers claiming 20 percent of overall sales (Rubenstein 1992). As Japanese automakers sought to overcome quotas limiting their exports to the United States, a potential consumer backlash against imported vehicles, and the cost of shipping finished vehicles across the ocean, they began building their own factories in the United States (Kenney and Florida 1994). These foreign-owned auto plants located in the United States, and assembling vehicles for the U.S. domestic market, are known as "transplant" factories. Led by Honda and Toyota, by the end of the 1980s Japanese automakers had the capacity to assemble more than two million cars and employed over thirty thousand workers in the United States.[4]

Whereas Japanese automakers added factories in North America throughout the 1980s as demand for their vehicles grew, U.S. domestic automakers closed plants because declining market share left them with production overcapacity. James Rubenstein (1992) calculates that the Detroit automakers closed twelve plants in the United States and Canada between 1979 and 1991, leaving them with fifty-seven.[5] But even these figures understate the sea change in market share under way in the industry. By 1991, GM, Ford, and Chrysler were actually operating twenty fewer plants assembling passenger cars than in 1979, a drop of 40 percent. Meanwhile, those three automakers increased the number of factories assembling light trucks and SUVs from eighteen to twenty-six, thereby increasing their reliance on the sale of large vehicles like those assembled in Silao, Janesville, and Arlington.

Throughout the 1990s and the first decade of the twenty-first century, automakers with foreign nameplates continued to expand their assembly capacity in the United States, typically in the South where there was minimal threat of unionization. Toyota, Honda, Nissan, BMW, Mercedes, Volkswagen, Hyundai, and Kia all opened factories. By 2008, there were thirteen domestic and foreign automakers assembling vehicles in the United States. The foreign transplants accounted for a full 30 percent of U.S. automobile production and employed over one hundred thousand people (Center for Automotive Research 2005). By contrast, the Detroit automakers shed nearly half a million jobs as they repeatedly downsized, restructured, and reorganized in an effort to regain their competitive traction and profitability. In 1978, Detroit automakers employed 667,000 hourly workers (*Philadelphia Inquirer*, September 8, 1996). By 2003, that number had fallen to 275,000 (*Detroit Free Press*, May 16, 2003). It would fall another one hundred thousand over the next five years (Rothstein 2008). Overall, the decline in market share enjoyed by the Detroit automakers and their efforts to cut overcapacity, combined with the influx of transplant factories, reshaped auto production in North America and blurred the distinction between what could be called "American" and "foreign" cars.

Globalization and the Spread of Lean Production

The process and impact of globalization ran deeper than just the integration of the continent with an expanded array of automakers. As new automakers, particularly Toyota and other Japanese automakers, gained market share and established manufacturing facilities in North America, they introduced lean production to the region. Though they first gained market share by offering inexpensive, fuel-efficient vehicles, Japanese automakers quickly earned a reputation for superior quality and efficiency. Their competitive advantage came to be seen as resulting not only from the products they offered but in the way they structured their companies and built their cars as well. Before long, an industry-wide restructuring was under way as the Detroit automakers shed their mass production philosophy to adopt lean production.

Unlike mass production, lean production calls for automakers to focus on their core competencies of automotive design, final assembly, and marketing. Rather than building cars from the ground up, lean production calls for the manufacture of parts, and whole components of cars, to be contracted to a network of parts suppliers with their own expertise who work closely with the automakers from a product's inception to its final production (Helper 1995; Helper, MacDuffie, and Sabel 2000). In reorganizing their firms, the automakers transformed their production role within the value chain from manufacturers to assemblers of automobiles (Rothstein 2005), placing greater emphasis on their responsibility for coordinating a supply chain of independent firms that manufacture an ever increasing percentage of the automobile, and often specialize in specific technologies or parts production (Veloso 2000). For the Detroit automakers, adopting lean production required shedding their vast networks of auto parts factories. GM consolidated many of its parts suppliers into Delphi Automotive Systems. Ford similarly created Visteon (Humphrey and Memedovic 2003). When the automakers spun off these divisions as independent auto part suppliers, they created the largest and second largest auto parts suppliers in the world, respectively.

On the shop floor, lean production revolutionized the organization of work. Though the roots of lean production lay in the standardization of work upon which mass production was based (Crowley et al. 2010; Tsutsui 1998), lean production systems are meant to harness workers' knowledge of the production process to improve productivity and quality, and therefore call for workers to be organized into teams and given opportunities to share and act upon their knowledge. Lean production systems are also designed to improve efficiency by persistently eliminating waste throughout the manufacturing process. Instead of building buffers into the manufacturing process as under mass production—by stockpiling parts, hiring extra workers, adding downtime to work routines—in order to ensure continuous production, lean production systems attempt to operate at the brink of collapse with ever slighter margins for error (Kenney and Florida 1993; Womack, Jones, and Roos 1990). This waste to be eliminated extends to the use of labor, certainly by cutting downtime, and arguably by creating a managerial imperative to exact increasing output from each worker, both mentally and physically (Babson 1995a; Dassbach 1996; Parker and Slaughter 1995).

The actual impact on work along the assembly line is a hotly contested debate that will be explored in the next chapter. What is undeniable is that the implementation of lean production has been associated with a drive for greater labor flexibility on the shop floor than was typical under mass production, with fewer job classifications and work rules, less rigid seniority systems, a weakening of the distinction between supervisory and non-supervisory work, and an overall lighter footprint for unions. Therefore, the spread of lean production as part of the process of globalization had a significant impact on workers within auto plants.

Studying Labor in the Global Economy

Each of the plants in this study is a location at which GM's value chain touched down in the wake of the globalization of the North American auto industry. The plants in Janesville and Arlington were two of GM's factories that survived the transition. Many workers in these factories were old enough to have lived the experience. The plant in Silao was part of the movement by automakers away from the traditional industrial heartland around Mexico City to assemble vehicles for export to the United States. Workers in Silao owed their very jobs to the process of globalization. At all three plants, workers were engaged in the assembly of vehicles based on the lean production model that had swept the industry.

In the tradition of the extended case method (Burawoy 1998, 2009), this analysis treats each of the plants in Silao, Janesville, and Arlington as reflecting the broader trends in the globalization of the North American auto industry. And just as value chain studies of sweatshops link retailers in the United States to the most egregious abuses of labor in the global economy, this book offers an analysis of the dynamic by which globalization has compromised job quality in the auto industry. So while the book analyzes the organization of work and labor relations at three GM plants assembling nearly identical vehicles, it is also a comparison of job quality in the eras before and after the globalization of the North American auto industry.

Fieldwork for this project was spread over five years. I spent roughly six months in Silao and the surrounding area during 2002 and the beginning of 2003. Research in Janesville began in 2003. For six months, I spent several days a week in Janesville, a forty-mile drive from my home in Madison, Wisconsin. Visits tapered off to once or twice a week through much of 2004 and into 2005. I was motivated to study the Arlington plant by issues that became prevalent in the Silao-Janesville comparison, and the research was conducted over a four-week period during two visits in 2006 and 2007.

At each site, I gained access to the shop floor and observed the assembly process from its beginning in the body shop to its culmination in final assembly. Details of local labor relations and the way the GMS was implemented were culled from interviews with managers, union officials, and workers. At each plant, GM executives and union officials consented to semistructured interviews lasting from one to two hours, most of which were recorded. In Mexico, I also interviewed Guanajuato state officials and toured a dozen auto parts plants in Silao and the surrounding region, six of which were part of GM's Silao supply chain. Human resource managers showed me their operations and sat for semistructured interviews covering their business, its employees, salaries, training, job requirements, and labor relations.

I spoke with dozens of GM assembly-line workers, often in local restaurants and bars. Few of these conversations were recorded, and I rarely took notes. Mostly, I waited until I was in my car to record my recollections of conversations, while sometimes excusing myself to run to the bathroom to jot something down. I got to know a number of workers quite well. They invited me to their homes and introduced me to their families. One invited me to her wedding, another to a gun show and shooting competition. Moreover, they served as ongoing sources of information, people to whom I could return to check my facts and request further explanation.

As with all multisite ethnographic research, there is some unevenness in my sources from plant to plant. Union officials in Mexico were more inviting than their U.S. counterparts. They allowed me to attend their meetings, orientations for new workers, social events, and one painstakingly transparent union election held in GM's parking lot. They took me to their favorite bars and showed me where to get the best tacos. On the other hand, I had greater access to workers in the United States than in Mexico, as the latter were bused in and out of the plant gates. Some of the workers I spoke to in Silao were also understandably wary of a nonnative Spanish-speaking researcher probing their opinions of GM and their union. Finally, since the histories of the plants in Janesville and Arlington are keys to the analysis that follows, and memories are subjective and sometimes faulty, in both Janesville and Arlington I augmented my interviews with the accounts of the day as reported in the local newspapers.

Because this research was designed to compare plants assembling the same vehicles, this study of the North American auto industry does not include any fieldwork in Canada. Instead, since the U.S. and Canadian industries merged in the 1960s, I treat them as one in analyzing the subsequent globalization of the North American auto industry. Admittedly, this leaves unexplored the differences in the two countries' labor relations and the manner in which their respective autoworker unions responded to industry changes, especially after the Canadian Auto Workers union (CAW) broke away from the UAW in 1985 (Kumar and Holmes 1998).

The Argument and Outline of the Book

Together, these auto plants offer a troubling paradox. The pace of work in the auto industry has intensified while remuneration has declined. Yet the auto industry still offers among the best unskilled blue-collar jobs available. Hence, regardless of country or locality, policymakers offer automakers great incentives to keep factories open or build new ones, all in the name of maintaining or creating "good" jobs. In recent years, GM has sent state and local policymakers scrambling to cobble together competitive offers of tax incentives and infrastructure projects to keep factories like those in Janesville and Arlington from closing. When successful, they are likely to see an influx of transferees relocating just to keep working on an assembly line. Similarly, automakers can expect to be wooed with incentives to locate new facilities in cities such as Silao. Whether in Mexico or the United States, prospective employees then inundate the companies with applications because, regardless of location, firm, or union status, the autoworker still has one of the most stable, highly paid blue-collar jobs available. Perhaps had auto work been surpassed by some other, better set of jobs, the worsening terms of employment in the auto industry might be dismissed as the end of an era, a period of the twentieth century when the auto was king. Instead, the dynamics behind the decline of wages, benefits, and working conditions in the restructured auto industry sheds light into the way globalization is undermining the bargaining power of workers with even some of the best jobs the global economy has to offer.

The following chapters build this argument by linking each plant to the globalization of the North American auto industry, beginning on the shop floor and then moving into the realms of local and national labor relations. Chapter 2 compares the organization of work and working conditions in Janesville, Arlington, and Silao to demonstrate that at all three plants work was organized around carefully choreographed standardized routines. The evidence contradicts assertions that lean production necessarily depends on a workforce that contributes both its physical labor and intellectual input to maximize firm performance. Instead, the comparison illustrates that at each plant GM's lean production system hinged on the strict adherence to standardized work routines prescribed by scientific management (Taylor 1911). In fact, though the factory in Silao practiced teamwork and encouraged workers to contribute their intellectual input at far higher rates than in Janesville and Arlington, all three plants met GM's demands for ever increasing productivity and scored equally well on industry measures of product quality.

These findings strip away the veneer of win-win situations described in the lean production literature, in which a firm's competitive edge in the global economy is inextricably linked to the empowerment of workers, who, in turn, gain more interesting and engaging work. Instead, the comparison of assembly lines demonstrates a world of work in which the drive for productivity results in an overall intensification of standardized routines that limit workers' discretion on the assembly line and marginalizes their input off it. Work is becoming harder and increasingly monotonous.

Chapters 3 and 4 explain how labor's acquiescence to intensifying work was facilitated by the labor relations regime at each plant. Chapter 3 argues that in both Janesville and Arlington, GM gained concessions to work rules and workplace rights through whipsawing. As the automaker lost market share and faced an overcapacity of production, GM forced local plants to compete with one another to stay open. The manner in which each plant was whipsawed is recounted to illustrate the process by which workers and their unions relinquished control of the shop floor and acquiesced to declining working conditions. The chapter also explains that lean production had been more thoroughly adopted in Arlington than in Janesville due to the two plants' respective prospects for the future. With little hope for the long-term operation of their plant, the emphasis in Janesville was on getting cars out the door and delaying the plant closure that was widely seen as inevitable, and which eventually came to pass. In Arlington, both management and labor saw the plant as viable in comparison to other GM facilities with which they competed to stay open, and both sides saw an effective implementation of the GMS as key to that survival.

Chapter 4 explains how, at GM's factory in Silao, the automaker harnessed its power as a coveted employer to nurture consent for work along the assembly line by crafting a labor relations regime conducive to the demands of lean production. In Silao, GM carefully selected only those workers with the background and personal characteristics most conducive to the style of teamwork envisioned in the GMS. In addition, the automaker hand selected a union to represent the young workers in a manner that reinforced management's vision of teamwork and labor-management cooperation. Finally, GM extended its control over labor relations outside its own factory to craft a local labor relations regime in which the automaker and its suppliers conspired to divide the local workforce by sex and educational level, and to maintain a wage hierarchy among the firms, with GM perched at the top.

Chapter 5 places the local labor relations regime through which GM manufactured consent at the three plants within the broader context of labor's declining bargaining power in each country, which has also resulted in lower wages and benefits. In both the United States and Mexico, the collective bargaining process through which autoworkers gained middle-class incomes and improved working conditions, once encouraged through each country's national industrial relations system, has been undermined. The concessions in Janesville and Arlington occurred within an environment of shrinking union density among autoworkers in the United States that has also compromised wages and benefits. Likewise, in Mexico, lower wages have accompanied the shifts in automotive industrial relations toward regimes like that found in Silao.

The final chapter of the book applies the lessons learned to a broader debate over what can be done to promote globalization in a way that benefits workers. By contrasting the outcomes for workers in this study to those of German autoworkers, and briefly comparing the labor side agreement to NAFTA, the North American Agreement on Labor Cooperation, to the European Union's Social Charter, the book ends with an examination of what can be done to prevent good jobs from getting worse in the global economy.

2

The Intensification of Work under Lean Production

Two months after taking office in 2009, amid the economic crisis that would become known as the Great Recession, President Barack Obama formed an Auto Industry Task Force to address the collapse of the U.S. domestic auto industry. The task force would eventually usher GM and Chrysler through bankruptcy proceedings. Explaining his decision to intervene, President Obama explained on the CBS program *Face the Nation* that "we think we can have a successful U.S. auto industry. But it's got to be one that's realistically designed to weather this storm and to emerge at the other end much more lean, mean, and competitive than it currently is" (March 29, 2009).

Exactly what the president meant in coupling the words "lean" and "mean" is open to interpretation. It may be that he was drawing on the common cliché "lean, mean, fighting machine" to drum up support for government intervention to save the automakers. Perhaps he was envisioning more efficient, less wasteful, "leaner" companies with attractive, "mean" product lines. Less likely is that the president was intentionally wading into the debate over whether or not lean production is "mean" to autoworkers, a key to determining whether or not job quality has declined due to globalization.

The debate over the impact of lean production on assembly-line workers began almost immediately after the term was popularized by the publication of *The Machine That Changed the World* (Womack, Jones, and Roos 1990), which describes the Toyota Manufacturing System as a paradigmatic shift away from the mass production system practiced by the Detroit automakers. And if Toyota was lean, then General Motors was fat. In fact, Toyota's manufacturing system was devised, in part, by studying GM's mass production system and determining how that system could be made more efficient (Fujimoto 1999).

For scholars taking what Steven Vallas (2006) labels the "human resource" or "post-Fordist" approach, there is nothing threatening to workers about lean production (Adler 1995; Kenney and Florida 1993; MacDuffie and Pil 1997). Instead, they describe a win-win scenario for management and labor alike as firms abandon the deliberate separation of the conception and execution of work prescribed by Frederick Winslow Taylor (1911) and achieved through mass production systems that left workers with no control over the assembly process (Braverman 1974). Instead, lean production *"transfers the maximum number of tasks and responsibilities to those workers"* (Womack, Jones, and Roos 1990, 99; italics in original). Theoretically, therefore, workers' intellects are reengaged under lean production, and the "mind-numbing stress" experienced under mass production is replaced by a "creative tension" (1990, 101–2), providing more "fulfilling work for employees at all levels" (1990, 225). All the while, workers participating in the Japanese principle of *"kaizen,"* or continuous improvement, help detect defects and eliminate wasted time, labor, parts, and money so the firm becomes more efficient and quality conscious.

These claims have been widely refuted by those who view "lean" as "mean" (Harrison 1994). The scholarship itself has been criticized for deducing positive effects of lean production on workers without empirical evidence from the shop floor (Graham 1995; Milkman 1997). Such studies of work gave rise to an alternative, hegemony perspective (Vallas 2006), which sees teamwork and other elements of lean production as manipulating workers to work harder and faster, actually enlisting them in their own exploitation (Babson 1995a; Dassbach 1996; Dohse, Jurgens, and Nialsch 1985; Fucini and Fucini 1992). So while lean production is wrapped in the language of "teamwork" and "empowerment," it is actually a speedup of the assembly line that compromises workers' long-term interests, safety, and health (Parker and Slaughter 1995).

This academic debate over the true nature of lean production and its impact on workers waned by the late 1990s. Neither side convinced the other, and scholars moved on to other topics. But the arguments of lean enthusiasts are periodically resurrected by conservative commentators to explain what they see as declining demand for unions by workers in the U.S. auto industry. Writing in *U.S. News and World Report* during the 2008 crisis among the Detroit automakers, Michael Barone declared that "Taylorism is pretty much dead in our society," having been superseded by lean production "from Japanese automakers who managed their plant not according to Taylorism but by giving their workers more autonomy and more responsibility—by treating them like sentient human beings and not like dumb animals as Frederick Taylor taught." Therefore, the labor unions that were once "seen as the necessary antidote to Taylorism" are outdated in an era of "Japanese management [that] requires cooperation between managers and workers" (Barone 2008). Following the same logic, Fred Barnes, executive editor of the *Weekly Standard*, applauded as "progressive anti-unionism" the strategies by which foreign automakers opening plants in the United States combat efforts to unionize their facilities (Barnes 2008).

But do these claims reflect workers' experiences on the assembly line? Lean production has become ubiquitous in the auto industry, adopted and adapted in one way or another by all major automakers as the successor to mass production (Vallas 1999). Yet, in spite of a broad literature on lean production, definitive answers have been elusive, at least in part for methodological reasons. Though studies of lean production in the auto industry abound, the variations in automakers and products mostly only allow for comparisons of lean practices and efforts to explain the differences (Boyer et al. 1998; Durand, Stewart, and Castillo 1999b; Kochan, Lansbury, and MacDuffie 1997; Liker, Fruin, and Adler 1999). A comparison of the plants in Silao, Janesville, and Arlington controls for several variables. All were owned and operated by GM. They assembled a similar array of vehicles built on the same platform, and some of the same makes and models. Furthermore, as at all GM assembly plants, the three factories were under orders to adopt an identical lean production system, though there was variation in the implementation between the plants. Comparing their three different interpretations of the GMS facilitates the identification of the core components of the manufacturing system as well as its common impact on workers.

Understanding the GMS is also particularly salient to the debates over the impact of lean production on auto work because the GMS was based directly on the Toyota Manufacturing System that became the archetype for lean production. GM learned lean production from Toyota at New United Motor Manufacturing, Inc. (NUMMI), the two automakers' joint venture that began in 1984 and lasted more than two decades. Toyota ran the plant in Fremont, California, under a special labor contract negotiated with the UAW that eliminated traditional seniority and work rules (Adler 1999). GM then applied the lessons learned from Toyota to devise the GMS. As the personnel director in Janesville explained, the GMS "is basically the old Toyota production system" that became the inspiration for lean production, but, according to the Janesville plant planner, "to put some ownership in it, it's called GMS—Global Manufacturing System." So the GMS is a direct descendent of the manufacturing system originally dubbed "lean production."

At issue are a few interrelated questions. What drives the lean production assembly line and how does this affect work? In what ways is it similar to, and different from, work under mass production? Most important, what has been the effect on job quality? Has the shift to lean production enhanced work by making it more cerebral and intellectually challenging? Or has work become harder, and why?

Research at the three plants revealed a broad consensus among supervisors, workers, and union officials that the key to the GMS was a meticulous standardization of work that allowed the automaker to keep workers in near constant motion. In fact, assembly-line work under lean production appears more routinized than it was under mass production, with the standardization of work facilitating an intensification of the pace of that work. GM's benchmark at all the plants was to keep line operators working for fifty-five seconds of each minute. In Silao, and to a lesser extent in Arlington, teamwork, job rotation, and employee participation schemes were implemented to facilitate and reinforce the standardization of work.

To tease out the importance of standardized routines under lean production and the resulting intensification of work, this chapter compares the implementation of the GMS in Silao, Janesville, and Arlington. While the comparison reveals that all three plants standardized work in nearly identical fashion, the factories differed sharply in the degree and manner in which they adopted techniques intended to engage workers' intellects. In Silao, these were implemented wholesale, and in Arlington, less so. In Janesville, on the other hand, teamwork and participation were implemented so superficially that some would argue that the plant was not operating a lean production system at all. However, I contend that it was—precisely because the key to the GMS is the standardization of work found in all three sites. To back up that claim, I offer productivity and quality measures indicating that the three plants performed equally well, which would clearly not be the case if teamwork and employee participation were the key to lean production.

With the importance of standardized routines to the lean production assembly line established, the chapter concludes by clarifying the nature of the shift from mass to lean production, and the impact on job quality. I'll argue that the claims of lean advocates that Toyota rediscovered and reengaged workers' intellects hinges on a mischaracterization of mass production as embodying the separation of the conception and execution of work. In reality, workers always used their brains on the assembly line. Instead, it seems apparent that Toyota's breakthrough was in appropriating workers' knowledge of the manufacturing process and using that knowledge to eliminate persistent defects. Ironically, smoothing out the kinks in production facilitates greater standardization of work, and, over time, reduces opportunities for workers' initiative. Advances in engineering and computer design leave even less need for worker input, while empowering management to ever more carefully synchronize activity on the assembly line and intensify the pace of work.

Lean Production at GM: The Global Manufacturing System Compared

In the years since the publication of *The Machine That Changed the World* (Womack, Jones, and Roos 1990), a broad literature has documented the spread of lean techniques throughout the auto industry, and lean production has lost its specific reference to Toyota.[1] Still, some changes to the organization of work are generalizable. In the process of becoming leaner, automakers have stopped stockpiling inventories of parts as they did under mass production. Instead, parts are delivered by suppliers on a "just-in-time" basis, arriving at the plant as close as possible to the time they will be needed on the assembly line. On that assembly line, workers are organized into teams that work together under the guidance of coworkers who serve as "team leaders" or "team coordinators," which has facilitated a reduction in the number of supervisors on the shop floor. Whereas under mass production, defective cars were repaired at the end of the assembly process, thereby allowing a systemic problem to affect all the vehicles on the line, lean production systems provide workers a means for halting assembly if they detect a defect so that the problem may be addressed, traced to its source, and resolved. Theoretically, a bad product should never be sent to the next team on the assembly line. Furthermore, procedures are in place through which workers are encouraged and expected to recommend changes to the design of vehicles, their parts, the assembly process, or the plant as a whole that will improve the efficiency of assembly and product quality.

In spite of the expanded role for workers, the tightly synchronized assembly process that facilitates just-in-time production under lean production requires that the assembly process remain highly standardized, if not even more standardized than it was under mass production. In fact, experiments with substantive participation (Levine and Tyson 1990) that empowered teams of workers to make decisions over the production process at Volvo (Berggren 1992) and GM's subsidiary Saturn (Cornette 1999; Rubinstein and Kochan 2001; Shaiken, Lopez, and Mankita 1997) were eventually discontinued due to their relative lack of productivity. Instead, under lean production, input from workers on the assembly line is generally consultative (Levine and Tyson 1990), encouraged as formal proposals for improving the way a job is done that, if accepted by management, then redefines the way all workers will perform that job (Vallas 1999).

On paper, the GMS incorporated all these characteristics of lean production: the standardization of work, the organization of workers into teams with team leaders, Andon systems to allow workers to stop the assembly line and address problems "in-station" so that no bad product moved further down the assembly line, and employee participation programs to solicit ideas for improving the lean system. To ensure implementation, GM had a "Core Requirements Tracking System," an eighty-five-page spreadsheet listing 263 items on which the plants were evaluated as green, yellow, or red. As Janesville's plant planner explained: "There are a lot of different systems within GMS, and they come in and they rate us and give us an evaluation and tell us where we're at with all the different items and elements in each major block of the GMS principles. So, we are compliant in every single category. It's just that some of them you have green, yellow, and red as far as states of implementation. Green meaning you're right there. Yellow meaning you're close. And red meaning you don't show a lot of progress or you're way behind." In spite of this tracking system and each plant's apparent success in meeting GM's standards, Silao's embrace of the GMS far exceeded the two plants in the United States, and especially that of Janesville, in every area except the standardization of work.

Standardization of Work

Of the various components of lean production, the one being fastidiously implemented at all three plants in this study was the meticulous standardization of work. At each work station in Janesville, Arlington, and Silao, the steps of assembly to be performed, and the order and manner in which they had to be completed, were documented as a production "footprint." As explained by a manager in Arlington:

> Every job that we have in this facility, whether it is in material or whether it is out here on the frame line, there is a standardized listing of every element of that job, and the specific sequence that you are supposed to perform that job in, and the amount of time that is allotted to do that job. And we have that level of detail for every job that is out there. If you are going to move any of those . . . there is a formalized process that is called an OCP or Operational Change Process, and IE [industrial engineering] maintain those standardized work sheets.
>
> Standardized work just basically says "here is how you do this job, and you do this job this way every time." And that is, if you pick up three bolts and put them here—you pick up three bolts and put them there. That is the first thing you do. And you do that the same way every time. Where you run into some quality issues is when people start deviating from their standardized work. . . . The next thing you know you've got missed work, or a screw not shot, or something like that because they deviated from the standard work and got out of process. Standardized work is just: "this is the way you do it and you do it like that every time."

Standardization not only ensured quality, but efficiency as well. Each task to be performed was assigned a specific number of seconds in which it had to be completed. Careful time studies like those conducted by Taylor (1911), aided by computer modeling, allowed GM to carefully calibrate each line operator's movement to keep them busy on one vehicle until the next one reached their work station. The mix of models and options on each assembly line complicated the process of filling each footprint with fifty-five seconds of work out of the minute cycle. A manager in Arlington emphasized this point:

> That's something that a lot of people lose sight of when you talk about different models that you build. There is option content with all those models.... You may do this on a Yukon. Tahoe, that's pretty similar. Then you throw in a Cadillac Escalade, obviously pretty different. Then you throw in some long wheel base—Suburban and Yukon XLs—they're different. So you have to balance that. Throw in a four-wheel drive, a lot different than a two-wheel drive. DVD entertainment system versus no entertainment system, sunroofs, off-road packages . . . that line moves at a steady rate. Yet every vehicle coming down that line is different . . . and all that being said, the benchmark is still fifty-five seconds.

For workers, the standardized routines were a far cry from intellectually stimulating. "Boring," "repetitive," "monotonous," and "mind-numbing" were some of the descriptions line operators at all three plants used to describe their work. And while the young workers in Silao who knew no other manufacturing system said little about the pace of work, the fifty-five-second benchmark was a speedup for many of the more experienced workers in the United States, and one that gradually deteriorated their working conditions. The union shop chairman in Janesville, the highest elected union official in the plant, explained that "I remember when I hired in, I could run up to the bathroom between jobs. You had to hustle, but you could make it and run back down and catch the next job, but not no more." The president of Local 95 in Janesville likened this continuous need to be at one's work station to "being in a cage."

One team coordinator in Arlington compared a day's work to running a marathon: "Every day that you work in that plant, you're gonna run a marathon, because every second of every minute is taken up by that job. So you have to be healthy. Mentally, too. If you're gonna go run the

Boston Marathon with the mind-set that you're not gonna make [it], you're not gonna make it. When you start that eight- or nine-hour shift, you gotta make it. If you got a sprained ankle, or carpel tunnel, or you're sick, it could break you." Likewise, in Janesville, one union commit-teeperson, whose role in the union was to represent workers on the shop floor, expressed his frustration that the public doesn't understand that "these guys work damn hard for fifty hours a week, and anyone who says otherwise don't know shit! My definition of 'lean' is fifty-five minutes out of the hour." He said that unlike the days when workers brought reading material to the assembly line, GM wanted line operators working "right there whistle to whistle," adding with chagrin that "the company ain't paying you to read. The company ain't paying you to stand around. It's hard to argue with."

Managers in Arlington made it plain that from their perspective there was nothing to argue about because, unlike in the past, under the GMS they conducted time studies to settle all questions about workload. One explained:

> If you go back in years within the UAW and General Motors, if an operator thought they were being asked to do more than a fair day's work, that was quite subjective. Today it is very objective. We know it takes four seconds to do this, twelve seconds to walk and pick this up, eight seconds to shoot that screw, four seconds to put that label on. . . . Now, you can dispute whether or not that time is right. That's fine. If you think there is an issue that we have not assigned an appropriate amount of time, we'll send an IE [industrial engineer] out there with a stopwatch and a clipboard and we need to validate.

Many line operators did not see it quite so simply, insisting that there was too little consideration for the people performing these tasks. One recent retiree in Janesville whose wife still worked in the plant made a typical complaint that the GMS was all about "young engineers" with their "computer models" who never worked on the assembly line but pestered workers with "can't we just add this one element? Can't you just do this one little thing?" He explained that "Sure you can, once or twice. But all day? And then they speed the line up, and look out!" His frustration turned to anger as he described the way the engineers treated the workers as though they were machines, losing any sense of their human needs or the hetero-geneity of the group. He suggested that somebody should sit these "kids" down and ask: "Have you factored in there that I might need a drink of water? Have you factored in there that I might need to tie my shoe? Have you factored in that I might be a person that needs to drink more water than the average person?"

Other workers complained that the tightly synchronized routines posed ergonomic challenges that could be exacerbated if a worker did not match the weight and height parameters GM's industrial engineers used in modelling jobs. A woman in Arlington pointed out that in her factory all the jobs were set up on the assumption the person performing it was right-handed, leaving her fewer jobs she could handle as a left handed person. Ultimately, one worker summed up work under lean production by saying "the assembly line is a hard way to make a living. The mental stress due to the monotony is bad enough, but the repetitive motion of bending the same way all day is worse."

Though workers in both Janesville and Arlington expressed frustration and anger about the manner in which the pace of work had increased over recent years, they implemented the standardized work routines just as workers did in Silao. But aside from this universal standardization of work, the three plants differed sharply in their implementations of all the other aspects of the GMS. In Janesville, both management and labor generally rejected teamwork and employee participation. In Silao, they were adopted wholesale. In Arlington, implementation of teamwork and participation was an ongoing process. But in Silao and Arlington these elements of the GMS were implemented with a focus on reinforcing or improving the standardization of work.

Table 2.1 compares the three plants' implementations of each of these elements of the GMS.

Teamwork

Among the changes lean production brought to the assembly line, perhaps none is supposed to be more consequential than the reorganization of workers into teams. Teamwork is meant to collectivize work and responsibility for a portion of the assembly process among a group of workers. Ideally, team members rotate among the different jobs within the team, which eliminates the distinction between "good" jobs and "bad" jobs and provides ergonomic relief. The personnel director in

Table 2.1
**Implementation of the key components of
the Global Manufacturing System (GMS)**

	Silao	Arlington	Janesville
Teamwork	Highly functional teams of five workers plus team leader; workers rotate jobs and perform administrative tasks	Semifunctional teams of six workers plus team coordinator	Superficial teams of four workers plus team coordinator
Role of team leaders/ coordinators	Quasi-supervisory role coordinating team activities; absentee and break replacement	Small coordinating role; absentee and break replacement	No coordinating role; mostly for break replacement
Andon system	Fully implemented triggering team-based problem solving	Implemented to alert team coordinator for assistance	Use discouraged by supervisors
Employee participation/input	Encouraged in all aspects of the plant	Encouraged with emphasis on cost reductions	Little used

SOURCES: Compiled from interviews with managers, workers, and union officials at each of the plants.

Janesville spoke of the importance of job rotation in distinguishing between teamwork and the traditional mass production approach he hoped to overcome: "It's a cultural issue to get them [the workers] to understand that you're a member of a team—you don't have job ownership. The team has ownership over these four jobs, as opposed to me having ownership of this particular stool or this particular job address. The idea is that everybody would get a chance to do all four jobs. So, it is a natural leveling. So, I don't sit back and say 'I don't want this element. Put it over there.' So, we load up that job and then the only person who has to do that job is the youngest person."

Typically, teams include a team leader, usually referred to as the "team coordinator" or "TC" at GM's factories in the United States. Theoretically, teams were supposed to become self-regulatory, with team coordinators assuming responsibilities that under mass production were the exclusive domain of management, thereby allowing the firm to operate with less shop-floor supervision. The personnel director in Janesville laid out just such a vision:

The team coordinator should really run the day-to-day business amongst his four team members, as far as rotation amongst the four, making sure that no vehicle leaves his station of the floor without being fixed. He's there to assist the team members when they pull the Andon cord and request help. He's there to make sure that the jobs are set up correctly, that the safety gear is in place.... He's there to provide some short-term absentee replacement coverage. These are all in the ideal state. He's there to do some torque checks, there to help write job instruction sheets and do job balancing between the four [team members], as well as to assist team leaders on either side of his team. He's the first responder when an employee would pull the Andon cord, and he would make the decision with the employee if it can be fixed in the station or whether they tag it and ship it to repair—whether it goes down the line or whether it be caught with a flag on the repair ticket so the downstream operators know that there is something amiss with that particular item or product.

Of the three plants, it was the one in Silao that came closest to implementing this version of teamwork, while in Janesville the reality of teamwork bore little resemblance to the ideal described by their personnel director.

Teamwork in Silao

In Silao, teams were composed of six workers, including the team leader. Each team occupied a particular "zone" of the assembly line encompassing five different work stations. The personnel relations manager described a zone as "the team's business unit, and they have a good idea how to work together. They are masters of this portion" of the assembly line, "and all of them should know about its operations" because team members maintained a regular rotation of their work on the line. A former process control manager, who had worked at both the Janesville and Silao plants, described the benefits of job rotation for workers in Silao: "They rotate their footprints. So, I might start out the beginning of the day at the first footprint within our team, and throughout the day we're going to rotate those jobs. So, you basically get to do a different job throughout the day instead of the same repetitive thing over and over. That's neat. . . . So, ergonomic relief is wonderful." He also emphasized that job rotation helped ensure quality because workers knew what their coworkers further down the line were doing, and the consequences of passing along faulty work: "Customer supplier interface is very good—internal customer supplier interface. The part that you're putting on as it goes down the line, how you put it on, how that work content is done, impacts that later footprint in many cases. So, by rotating, you understand your customer very well, because at times you are the customer and at times you're the supplier, as far as how the build goes. So that's a unique thing that I've never seen in a car company before—where people rotate."

In addition to rotating through each job in the team's zone, the plant's "Points of the Star" system required each production worker to assume an administrative task associated with one of five points of a star. Through this system, the teams monitored their own productivity, safety record, the training of each worker on each footprint, and the cost of the parts they used and the scrap they created.

At the center of the star was the team leader responsible for managing and coordinating all the team's work. Team leader positions were quasi supervisory. On the one hand, team leaders were members of the team who were expected to work on the assembly line and be prepared to cover the work at any footprint within their zone. On the other hand, they were administrators, coordinating and overseeing the team's work and the training of new team members, and communicating with plant management. One line operator in Silao described his team leader like this:

> He supports everyone. If someone is absent, he steps in. If someone goes on vacation, he steps in. . . . When his team is complete, he is in charge of making sure everyone has time to do their job, of ensuring quality, of implementing plans to eliminate discrepancies or defects, of keeping his team in good condition. . . .
>
> He is the sanity of the team, addressing work issues to keep the team productive and quality conscious, financial issues to check the list of materials with the finances to make sure they are in order. This is what the leader does. He supports everything.

The selection of team leaders was a thorough process involving both managers and the line operators in the teams themselves. Vacancies were posted in the plant. Applicants were required to have at least a year of employment, no absences in the previous year, a clean disciplinary record, and no history of workplace accidents. After leadership training, aspiring team leaders were interviewed by the team in need of a new leader. The personnel relations manager explained that, hypothetically, "ten apply. . . . Those who go to the course and take a technical exam—three pass. And these three interview with a work team, and the team judges them. So, now we have two screenings."

He further indicated that efforts were made to promote team leaders from within a team, but that this was not always the case. Some teams did not have members who were ready. Also, management did not want to prevent a worker from becoming a team leader just because his team had a stable leader. GM wanted team leaders to hold their position in perpetuity. The personnel relations manager emphasized that the goal for teams was that "they are permanent. They are stable. And the stability is something that we try to maintain because the team works well. After a certain time they know very well, in general, the business."

Teamwork in Janesville

By contrast, teams in Janesville were strictly pro forma, resembling a style that has been labeled "Fordist" because the roles workers play are similar to those under mass production (Durand, Stewart, and Castillo 1999a). Workers were technically organized into teams of five, including a team coordinator, but these were merely groupings of consecutively placed workers on the assembly line. Unlike team members in Silao, line operators in Janesville did not perform any administrative tasks. Furthermore, job rotation was nonexistent due to a plant-wide seniority system through which workers claimed ownership over a specific footprint, and could transfer to a different job up to three times a year (1999 Local Agreement between UAW Local 95 and General Motors Truck Group Janesville, Wisconsin: Section VI, 6). For workers, the goal was to gradually move to easier work on the assembly line as one aged, and then land a job off the assembly line. Moving off-line typically meant first taking a job in material handling, delivering parts to the assembly line. If a worker accumulated enough seniority, more than thirty years in Janesville, they might be fortunate enough to land a job completely free of the pressure associated with production, perhaps in "unskilled maintenance" sweeping up and cleaning bathrooms. One line operator joked that you could identify the worker with the most plant seniority because they would be outside mowing the small strip of grass in front of the plant.

Workers in Janesville viewed the seniority system as a hard-won, inviolable right that protected older workers from the rigors of the assembly line. As a result, any mention of job rotation was met with opposition. As the union's shop chair indicated, "If I got eighteen years' seniority, and you've got two years, I don't want to rotate to your job. That's why you got it. Right, wrong, or indifferent." One woman with low seniority, who would arguably benefit from job rotation, emphatically argued, "that would ruin the whole seniority system. The idea of the seniority system is that you get to work less and you get easier jobs as you get older." Pointing to one of her coworkers, she questioned, "I've got nine years in. He's got twenty-four. Why would he want to rotate with me?"

Even for the plant's personnel director, who described GM's vision for teamwork and was responsible for negotiating the local collective bargaining agreement with the union, the idea of actually implementing job rotation was so remote that the notion of how it would work in Janesville remained vague:

> In a pure GMS environment, they would rotate as a matter of course. Now, the duration in which they rotate might be once a week. I might do your job for Monday, and his job for Tuesday, and his job for Wednesday, and do my own on Thursday. Or, we may rotate at each break. I do your job for a couple of hours today, and then that job and that job, and then my own. Or, any combination in between. The rotation has got to be such that you can change places so it's got to happen at a natural time when you can walk up and down the line—but it could be at break and it could be at lunch and it could be the next day.

With teams merely an administrative formality, the role assumed by team coordinators in Janesville bore little resemblance to the job of team leaders in Silao. Instead, team coordinators appeared responsible for little more than spelling workers who needed a break to go to the bathroom, get a drink, or handle personal business. In fact, when specifically asked what team leaders do, workers repeatedly responded with some variation of "they give me a break so I can go to the bathroom." For workers, the difference between good and bad team coordinators was often a simple matter of the frequency with which they provided such relief and how immediately they responded to requests. One team coordinator described his role as "to take care of my people." Another indicated that "I take care of my people pretty good" by making sure they get three bathroom breaks a day and not making it a hassle if they needed more. One worker, a self-described "day trader before there were day traders," raved that his team coordinator allowed him a daily morning break to check the market and phone in his trades.

A few team coordinators were beginning to take on administrative duties, as envisioned by plant management, but these were preliminary and isolated cases. Others resisted. One TC expressed her concern that if she was expected to manage the team more thoroughly, she would be put in a position of coordinating the team's vacation and other leave, ultimately granting and denying workers' requests for time off. That was a role she viewed as strictly managerial, saying, "I don't want that responsibility. I don't want to be anyone's boss." Another echoed the concerns of scholars (Dassbach 1996; Parker 1993; Parker and Slaughter 1995) that teamwork was about "trying to create peer pressure in the plant" by getting team coordinators to cross the line between the concerns of supervisors and workers. She said they would resist, because "we have enough issues. We don't need to take on management issues."

An additional obstacle to team coordinators expanding their role was the manner of their selection. While team leaders in Silao were jointly selected by management and team members and trained to serve a quasi-supervisory role, in Janesville team coordinators selected the role themselves through the seniority system. The only requirement was sufficient seniority, and many team coordinators selected the post specifically to get off the assembly line rather than to assume greater responsibilities. According to the personnel director, this would need to change to have effective teams: "Right now they are selected by application and in a seniority order fashion. So, we currently select from amongst the oldest right now. Providing they can do the job, they get the job. We would like a selection process that judges their skills and abilities a little more, and then gives consideration to seniority, so that we are sure that we are going to get the right type of person to be a coordinator/leader."

At the time, though, they appeared to be heading in the opposite direction. In 2002, a year before I began this research, Janesville lost a small assembly line building medium-duty work trucks when GM moved production to a plant in Flint, Michigan. Eight hundred jobs were lost as a result. Rather than lay off the least experienced workers in a traditional "last in-first out manner," local management and union officials negotiated an "inverse layoff." Workers with the most seniority were given the option of going into the "jobs bank," a provision of the national collective bargaining agreement through which laid-off workers were paid their full wage while they waited to be recalled by the automaker. (The jobs bank was discontinued in 2009 as part of GM's bankruptcy restructuring.) But once these high-seniority workers were called back to work, they did not return to the jobs they had left. Rather, they had to select among those positions that were available, typically the most physically demanding on the assembly line.

The widely perceived intention of the inverse layoff was to encourage older workers to retire rather than rejoin the assembly line. Most had already accumulated the thirty years' seniority they needed to qualify for a full pension. The inverse layoff would let them "get their feet wet in retirement without actually making a commitment to retirement," as one worker put it. While several hundred of those who accepted the inverse layoff did retire, others were returning to the plant after more than a year away, accepting jobs on an assembly line that moved much faster than when they last staffed it, and often faster than they could handle. One recently returned line operator with thirty-five years' seniority who had not worked on the assembly line itself in twenty years stated frankly, "The line moves too fast. I can't do the work."

The return of these older workers coincided with the implementation of the most recent local labor agreement that cut the size of teams in half, from eight to four workers. Therefore, the number of team coordinators in the plant was doubling just as these long tenured workers were returning, and they were snatching up the vacancies as a way of getting off the assembly line. More than a few line operators complained that their new team coordinators were reluctant to help out on the line. Instead of being viewed as leaders, they were widely resented for returning to work after the layoff instead of retiring, for taking the prized team coordinator positions, and for the way they performed the job as well.

Teamwork in Arlington

If Silao offers a model of work organized around fully functional teams, and Janesville a lesson in how teams can be superimposed over a production process without actually reorganizing work, the plant in Arlington offers an example of semifunctional teams negotiated into place. Teams in Arlington included six line operators and a team coordinator. A few teams had implemented job rotation for ergonomic reasons, but for the most part workers were responsible for only the specific job they selected through the seniority system. A human resource manager echoed his counterpart in Janesville while describing the difficulty of implementing job rotation in Arlington, and how he imagined it might eventually happen: "It's a long-standing issue with high-seniority employees that they've worked many, many years to get to the job that they consider a good job. However, if you can ever get there, and the true team concept is that . . . we balance those jobs so that idealistically there aren't any good jobs or bad jobs. There are level jobs. And you're going to rotate to all of them. So, you're going to have a vested interest in balancing that work. That's really team concept. That's what I think rotation helps drive."

In spite of the lack of job rotation, teams were more functional than in Janesville because the seniority system in Arlington promoted team stability, which appeared to foster team collegiality and cooperation. Unlike the plant-wide seniority system in Janesville, the seniority system in Arlington had been augmented so that vacant jobs were first available to other workers within the team. Once the team members had shifted into the positions they most desired, the remaining job became available to other workers in the plant.

This style of seniority system promoted team continuity and fostered ties among workers in the team, as well as greater familiarity with each other's jobs than in Janesville. As a result, line operators expressed greater willingness to informally help one another than in Janesville, where workers steadfastly observed the demarcations between jobs. As one team coordinator explained: "Say you and me work together for a year or two. We work next to each other. Maybe we're working on a tailgate together. I do part of the tailgate and then you come in right behind me and finish it. Well, you'll know what I do, and I'll know what you do. So in case of an emergency, and your team leader is not around, you're going to cover me or I'm going to cover you."

The team continuity promoted by the seniority system also affected the performance of team coordinators. They were among the most senior members of the team and had worked many of the different jobs in the team before becoming coordinator. They also knew the different members of the team. The team coordinator interviewed above indicated that this led him to take initiative in relieving workers on the line, both to give them a break and to maintain production:

> Sometimes I'll see one of my girls [*sic*] agitated. I've spent a lot of time on that line. I know. I know. I jump in and I tell them, "Take care. Go to the bathroom. Go get a cup of coffee. Relax. Relax a little bit." And they do. I'm a leader. I know . . . to get them off the line for a few minutes even though my job might suffer because of it. I'm still keeping the team functioning.
>
> You know when somebody is really agitated, because you have to cover their job a few times because they forgot something simple. If they were functioning properly, they'd never have to call you. I'd never have to do anything. But then that one night, they're screwing up. They cannot focus on that job. So I have to take the time to cover them, and it's easier just to say "Get off the job and let me do it a while. Take a break."

In addition, team coordinators in Arlington assumed several responsibilities that their counterparts in Janesville did not. As in Silao, team coordinators in Arlington filled in for workers unexpectedly absent for the day. When a TC was working on the assembly line, the team coordinators on either side of the team split responsibility for that team, thereby increasing by 50 percent the number of workers under their watch. Team coordinators ran weekly team meetings, communicated with supervisors on behalf of the team, took the lead in resolving problems on the line, and ordered materials. They were also trained to set up, or "scroll" jobs, detailing on paper the tasks associated with each job when changes were made to the footprint, a role that appeared to sometimes put them in conflict with the industrial engineers' ideas for standardized work.

As in Janesville, the dedication and skill with which team coordinators performed their tasks varied. Managers suggested they would prefer the positions not be awarded by seniority, and claimed to be "in dialogue with the local union" over finding alternative criteria. The union leadership, however, indicated they would not leave it up to management's "judgment calls" and that it was GM's responsibility to train the higher seniority workers who "deserve the opportunity to lead a little bit." In the end, human resource managers indicated they were reaching consensus around a plan of "deselection—that if we have team leaders who are not fulfilling all of their roles and responsibilities, that there is a process and a means to remove them." Such a system of deselection would be typical of the way the GMS was negotiated into place in Arlington.

Andon Systems and Building In-Station

Another fundamental shift in manufacturing philosophy associated with the transition from mass production to lean production, which teamwork is supposed to facilitate, involves the role of the line operator as a guarantor of product quality. Whereas under mass production workers were considered either incapable or too unreliable to recognize and address product defects, under lean production workers are expected to insure product quality and to build in-station. Rather than let faulty products continue down the assembly line, workers are supposed to address the problems immediately, even if doing so requires that they stop the assembly line.

At GM's plants, building in-station was facilitated through the use of an Andon system. Under the GMS, a line operator experiencing a problem would pull an Andon cord found at each work station. Doing so triggered an alert for assistance and halted the assembly line in their zone. Ideally, the problem would then be addressed and the assembly line restarted before other work teams were affected. In practice, the sophistication of the Andon systems, and the manner in which they functioned, reflected the variation in teamwork practiced at the three factories.

The Andon System in Silao

In Silao, the Andon system harnessed the collective knowledge of the entire team, under the guidance of the team leader. As one worker described, "If you notice on the line there are cords. . . . This guy, this worker, if he has a problem—of quality, of whatever cause, that a tool isn't working, whatever cause—that you want to report, pull the cord. At the moment it is pulled, the sign lights up." He was referring to the overhead LCD signs throughout the plant that flashed the team's alphanumeric code when an Andon cord was pulled to alert everyone that "this is a work station. It's upholstery—station number 106—right side. Then, in the center of the line, there are little numbers and they light up, and the music starts playing." Each team was also designated a specific musical jingle that would start playing when the Andon system was triggered. "Then if the team leader is busy, . . . he hears the music and says 'oh, that's my team' and, boom! he runs to give support." Team members working at other footprints within the zone, or off the assembly line performing their administrative task, would likewise converge on the area to resolve the problem. Ideally, this was done quickly and the line restarted before causing a backup affecting other teams.

In using the Andon system, the goal was to get everyone back to their standardized work as quickly as possible. Even the process of group problem solving was standardized. Specifically, the work teams were trained to address Andon alerts through a step-by-step group problem-solving process known at the Seven Diamond Process. The first three steps were a checklist of relatively simple problems that commonly arise on an assembly line manufacturing several different models of cars, each with different options. Is the task being performed as directed by the footprint? If so, are the correct tools being used, and are they functioning properly? Have they been properly maintained? Or do they need repair? If the process and tools were not the problem, was the correct part being installed? If so, the workers could then involve a quality engineer to assist in determining if the parts being delivered met specifications and whether the vehicle should be pulled from the line.

If the workers proceeded through the first four steps of the Seven Diamond Process without correcting the problem, the process control manager would be summoned to determine whether to report the problem for consideration off the shop floor. But it was engineers, not line operators, who then performed the intellectually challenging final three steps of the Seven Diamond Process to determine whether an assembly process had to be reengineered, a part redesigned, or whether there was some other solution to a recurring problem. Most Andon pulls never reached this stage. Instead, the teams quickly resolved them in a matter of seconds, without any interruption to production.

The Andon System in Janesville

Just as the Andon system in Silao capitalized on the extensive use of teamwork in the plant, in Janesville and Arlington the Andon system reflected the relative functionality of their work teams. In both locations, team coordinators were technically assigned to take the lead in resolving problems on the assembly line. A worker experiencing difficulty was supposed to pull the Andon cord to alert his team coordinator, who would then quickly determine whether to address the problem or call a supervisor for assistance. The personnel director in Janesville described the process and benefit of the Andon system this way:

> The advantage of the Andon system . . . is that they [the line operators] determine whether they can fix something in-station. So, they are always shifting good work—always shifting a good truck. If they've got problems, they've got a cord that they can pull, and somebody will immediately respond—the team leader. So, the team leader responds and then those two guys put their heads together and decide, "OK, can I fix it? Can you fix it and I'll go back and do the next job? Can you continue on to the next job and I'll fix this here, being the leader? Or is it such a repair that we'll flag the ticket and we'll catch it at either the buyout stations or final repair?" . . . So, they could be having troubles with a particular bolt always cross-threading and all they're gonna do is write the job up until their supervisor comes along. Whereas with the Andon process, they call immediately and get immediate help, and hopefully immediate correction.

In practice, this description bore far greater resemblance to the process in Arlington than in Janesville.

In Janesville the Andon system had fallen into disuse. Workers overwhelmingly reported that their Andon calls did not trigger a response from team coordinators, but by supervisors who immediately reset the system and tagged the car for later inspection. Line operators consistently complained of their supervisors begging, exhorting, and demanding that they not disrupt production by pulling the Andon cord. "Don't shut me down!" was the refrain.

In fact, workers often cited the failure on the part of supervisors to properly implement the Andon system as evidence of management's lack of dedication to the principle of building in-station. One woman working in the paint department summed up the prevailing attitude this way:

> They can come right through and the foreman will tell you that "we're here for quality. Quality counts. Quality is our number-one priority." And then we'll have a breakdown, and all of a sudden "don't stop that line for nothing. If you can't get it, that's all right. Just let it go. They'll get it in the next area. Don't

worry about it. Don't shut down the line for any reason." All of a sudden when it comes down to the numbers, and the numbers are low, we don't want quality anymore. You get that truck out that door.

Moreover, workers complained that their supervisors were disinclined to investigate the root cause of systemic problems, which really did appear to frustrate workers as much as proponents of lean production claim in stressing the system's superiority over mass production (Kenney and Florida 1993; Womack, Jones, and Roos 1990). One line operator summed up a common sentiment among workers that management's attitude was "what can we do to get you to shut up right now? We'll zip your lip for today and when it [the problem] comes back in two days, we'll do the Band-aid again without getting to the real issue."

Line operators throughout the plant insisted that management's concern for costs, speed, and productivity often came at the expense of product quality, which they contended was far more important to the workers than it was to their supervisors. One line operator in the body shop complained that "there are a lot of quality-conscious people on that line. But management is under pressure to get them [the cars] out." Another described the plant management's overriding philosophy with regard to quality as "if you can't reach your goal, lower your standard. Number-one priority is numbers [of trucks], and it always will be. That's why the workers get frustrated and say 'fuck it.'"

This perception among workers that their supervisors preferred that they pass problems further down the assembly line rather than pull an Andon cord led many to simply ignore the Andon system to avoid the hassle. Others reported using the system to confront their supervisors. One team coordinator declared herself to be "a strong believer in the Andon system. It gives us ammunition" to demonstrate to management that they are giving line operators "too much work." She claimed that the goal of requiring fifty-five seconds of work for each minute left insufficient time to address quality and other production problems on the line. So she encouraged the members of her team to pull the Andon cord, and bragged that her team consistently led the plant in Andon calls. In fact, she claimed that her persistence had born exactly the type of results intended by the use of Andon systems. Her team had forced their supervisors to fix problems or face persistent downtime. As a result, her zone experienced a decline from roughly one hundred Andon calls a shift to only twenty-three. From her perspective, "if foremen are addressing issues, they don't have so many" Andon calls. But their reluctance to resolve problems can "get quite frustrating."

Supervisors' wariness of workers pulling the Andon cord was grounded in distrust and the reality that the Andon system could become a tool by which disgruntled workers registered their protests against the standardization and intensification of work they experienced. Some line operators in the plant spoke of coworkers who abused the system (though none claimed to do so themselves), thereby undermining the confidence of supervisors that workers could be trusted to use the Andon system. Others articulated a dynamic that Vallas (2006) describes as an "ongoing tension" between the "logic of *standardization*, born of the engineering thrust for predictable, calculable, and closely controlled methods of production" and "the logic of *participation* . . . to engage workers' commitment" (Vallas 2006, 1690; italics in the original). Andon cords were sometimes pulled when workers could otherwise easily fix a problem themselves, but doing so would require deviating from the standardized routine in their footprint. Instead, they pulled the chord to make a point. One worker described the mind-set: "Now, why would they make that line stop? Because they're overworked. They're abused. So they work to rule. You gonna screw me, I'll screw you back. I'll work to rule. I'll do what this job description says—no more, no less. . . . You are following the rules. They can't burn you. That's the only power we have, the working men and women."

So in Janesville, supervisors and line operators were caught in a vicious circle. Managers under tremendous pressure to maintain production did not trust workers to use the Andon system responsibly, which fueled the perception among workers that their supervisors cared more about keeping the line moving than quality, and caused some workers to behave in ways that reinforced management's distrust. Ultimately, this mutual distrust between supervisors and line operators led to a far less functional Andon system than in Silao. Workers mostly ignored the Andon system unless a problem arose that simply prevented them from performing their job at all, and supervisors responded with a high degree of suspicion that the system had not been triggered legitimately.

The Andon System in Arlington

Unlike in Janesville, workers and supervisors in Arlington appeared to have come to an understanding regarding the use of the Andon system. One recently retired worker indicated that "really it functions quite well." Team coordinators took the lead when the Andon cord was pulled and called a supervisor if they needed assistance. If the problem was not fixed by the end of the footprint, and the line stopped, at that point other team members would leave their posts to try to lend a hand. He emphasized that takes real teamwork.

Having worked in the plant for thirty-one years, the retiree also noted that implementing the Andon system was a "long and painful" process, and that "the first step in that was building the trust that if you stop the line you won't get fired. It starts at the top." At their introduction into a plant, Andon systems expose problems, many systemic, in great number. He said that "it was a great victory to get under one hour downtime a day," but by the time he left it was about five minutes, indicating that systemic problems had been eliminated as intended.

This is not to say the Andon system in Arlington matched Silao's. Line operators indicated that there was, at times, a "lack of commitment" from supervisors. Some problems were let go, and workers learned what to address and what to send down the line. It was also not unheard of for supervisors to reset the Andon system to keep the line moving and fix a problem later. It just did not happen to such an extent that the workers stopped using the Andon system altogether as in Janesville.

So while the Janesville plant demonstrates the precariousness of Andon systems and building in-station in low trust environments, Arlington shows that such trust can be negotiated into place. It does not have to be built from scratch as in Silao. Yet the factories in Silao and Arlington expose a real discrepancy between the theoretical benefits of adding an intellectual challenge to the assembly line and the reality of the way Andon systems function. For a plant to operate efficiently with an Andon system, that system has to be seldom used and problems quickly resolved. That is, the problem solving that is said to provide workers an intellectual challenge cannot be sufficiently complicated to provide that challenge routinely, or the factory would suffer low productivity. Instead, the Andon system as practiced in both Silao and Arlington, more often than not, served to get workers back to their standardized routines.

Employee Input

In addition to assuring product quality through Andon systems, under lean production workers are expected to participate in "*kaizen*," or "continuous improvement," by suggesting ways to increase productivity and safety, cut costs, or otherwise improve efficiency and plant performance. Premised on the notion that workers possess important information about the work they do, and that their knowledge should be a key resource for management, this aspect of lean production is said to be a decisive departure from Taylor's (1911) prescription for separating the conception and execution of work, lest workers use their knowledge to shirk their responsibilities on the assembly line. Instead, lean production encourages workers' input so that the standard by which work is performed can be improved (Womack, Jones, and Roos 1990).

Under the GMS, each factory had a consultative participation system (Levine and Tyson 1990) by which workers could submit to the automaker their ideas for improving their workplace. To encourage ideas that saved money, at all assembly plants GM offered bonuses of 20 percent of the calculated first-year savings associated with any recommendation workers made, up to $20,000 for ideas submitted by individuals and $25,000 for those from groups of workers. In addition, local managers had some discretion in distributing smaller awards, up to $1,000 for worthwhile ideas to which specific cost savings could not be directly attributed. As was the case with the functionality of work teams and the Andon system, the manner and degree to which plant management encouraged, solicited, and implemented the ideas offered by workers differed sharply.

"Ideas and Improvements" in Silao

In Silao, employee participation was designed as an extension of the plant's system of teamwork. Based on the data line operators maintained through their own record keeping and their experiences on the assembly line, workers submitted recommendations for improvements of a particular footprint, their zone of the assembly line, or the plant as a whole through a program called "Ideas and Improvements." The scope of the program, and management's expectations of workers, was described by the plant's personnel relations manager: "They participate in lean production. This is very important. . . . We have a system of Ideas and Improvements . . . for when they come up with an improvement to the process—to the cost, to productivity, to safety, etc., and they have a contribution of general savings. . . . This year, there was 85 percent participation. . . . The focus of this tool, this system, is improvement—the improvement of everything, not just cost. Cost is important. Right? But it's important to improve safety. Productivity is important; improvements in quality." Interviews revealed a wide range of recommendations, from the redesign of parts and the process of installing them, to simple ideas workers had for making their own jobs easier, by moving a stock of parts to reduce bending, for example. A few workers praised the Ideas and Improvements program for promoting ergonomics in just this way.

Other ideas resulted in significant savings and bonuses for the workers. According to the plant's daily information bulletin displayed as the centerpiece on each table in the cafeteria, in January 2003 one worker was awarded nearly $8,000 for suggesting the redesign of a shipping container, a tremendous bonus considering he earned less than $10,000 a year in wages. The previous packaging required workers who unloaded the parts from the delivery trucks to rotate in and out, leaving each worker with downtime as they waited their turn. During one such break, this individual envisioned a packing system that would allow the truck to be unloaded more efficiently and save money by eliminating the downtime. He used his bonus to open his own car wash to supplement his income from GM.

Beyond offering financial rewards, GM's managers in Silao promoted the Ideas and Improvements program by drawing attention to workers' recommendations that had been implemented. All the recommendations that had been approved in the previous month, thirty-two in December 2001, were documented on a large "*kaizen*" display in the center of the plant, including the original submission with the names of the workers who made it, a description of the outcome, and before and after photos. Also documented in this area were all the teams' performance measures, which allowed anyone to quickly compare their productivity, downtime, and waste.

According to one production engineer, line operators' suggestions were a regular and fundamental part of working out the kinks associated with annual model changes that required each teams' footprints to be redrawn to include their updated tasks. As the changes to the footprints were introduced, waves of recommendations for improvements flooded in from the work teams actually implementing the standardized routines designed by the plant's industrial engineers. Over a period of a couple of months, the number of recommendations would decrease as the teams settled into what appeared to be the most efficient work processes. So just as the Andon system in Silao was designed to get workers back to their standardized routines as quickly as possible, a primary purpose for soliciting workers' ideas was to achieve the most efficient standardized routine for each footprint.

Lack of Input in Janesville

While workers in Silao actively participated in recommending improvements to the production process, distrust between management and labor in Janesville caused the program for soliciting workers' ideas to fall into a similar state of disuse as the plant's Andon system. Workers reported that their ideas and advice went largely ignored, or languished. One line operator reported raising an issue repeatedly over a ten-month period, and that "nothing has happened, and it won't." A high-ranking union official in the plant indicated that when he worked on the assembly line he did receive a substantial bonus for recommending a design change to make a part easier to install. However, he expressed exasperation at having to resubmit the idea several times over almost an entire year before management acknowledged and implemented his recommendation.

Moreover, workers' experiences of the GMS as an intensification of work, reinforced by their supervisors' lack of commitment to the Andon system and building in-station, fed workers' skepticism over the participation scheme. Many openly questioned why they would contribute to making their own work more difficult. The union's shop chair insisted that GM was asking the union and the workers to cross a line between participating in the improvement of product quality and plant safety into a realm in which workers recommended to the automaker ways the company could cut jobs. He indicated that while he did not object to workers participating per se, plant management was not acknowledging the inherent conflict of interest embedded in the system:

> What's involved is giving the people on the floor more input into the daily running of the plant. They make each area into a little bitty team. That team, their job responsibility is a certain amount of jobs in that area. How can they make them better? How can we resolve quality issues? But management wants to come out and say, "We need to take a person out. How do you think we can

take a person out?" That's when we put the flag up. No, that ain't our job, to tell you how to eliminate people. They got their ulterior motives that are tied in there. They want the people to agree on how they're going to work harder.

Ultimately, he said, they would not be drawn into it, indicating that "we'll do GMS the Janesville way. It's not going to be the Lansing [Michigan] or Arlington way. It's not going to be the NUMMI way. It's going to be like Janesville. Think of the workforce. . . . People first."

Management in Janesville acknowledged that workers' ideas were not always respected nor fully acknowledged. The former process control manager with experience in both Silao and Janesville indicated that two very different attitudes toward worker participation were in play. In Silao, employees' recommendations were accepted as an important component of improving the production process. By contrast, in Janesville the norm was to depend on engineers to design the assembly process. Therefore, recommendations were not received with open minds by managers in Janesville, who expected that "everything is done from the outside [of the plant]. It's basically, 'ergonomics—well, we've got ergonomics engineers out there.' If you have a problem you get ahold of an ergonomics engineer and study the problem independent of the person actually doing the work."

He further explained that management and labor in Janesville were caught in a vicious circle around worker' suggestions. Management was skeptical of workers' recommendations precisely because they understood that workers experienced the GMS as an intensification of their labor. As a result, processing the recommendations submitted by workers in Janesville was of low priority and took much longer than in Silao. Frustrated workers reinforced management's low expectations by stuffing the suggestion boxes with anonymous, often profanity-laced complaints. He said that workers also used the system to air complaints that had nothing to with production, for instance by putting "in a suggestion that says 'Put a sign by the drinking fountain that says, "No spitting."'" So, they just clog it [the suggestion box] with all sorts of stuff" that made sifting through the recommendations more of a chore than it was usually worth.

During the process control manager's time working in Janesville, he saw that workers also played the system, looking for opportunities to demand bonuses for ideas that were not their own: "Oftentimes, people along the line will see me or one of my problem solvers working on fixing a problem. And they'll see kind of what we're doing and they'll write a suggestion on it and put it in before we're done with what we're doing. And then they can say, 'Aha! Look. I had this suggestion in before you guys figured it out for yourselves. So pay me. What are you gonna pay me?' There's a lot of that that happens."

Since his own job required workers to assist him in implementing changes, he would further play the system, currying workers' favor by tipping them off that he was going to implement a change so that they could claim recognition for his ideas, even though he realized doing so further undermined the integrity of the overall system. As he recalled: "I did one project, and I'm supposed to have a champion—someone on the management team that sanctions my project. But they wouldn't buy off on it. So I just kind of went and did it on my own because I knew it was the right thing to do. I found the solution and went to my four problem solvers that worked for me. I said, 'Here, put a suggestion in on this.' And they got $25,000 out of that. I knew what it was for me. I was buying their loyalty. Because you need people like that. Plus, who cares? It's not my money."

Again, just as with their implementation of the Andon system, distrust between workers and management led to an ineffective participation program. Management understood the link workers made between recommending improvements and the intensification of work expressed by the union shop chair. The former process control manager summed up workers' attitudes toward even those ideas that might make their own work easier. He figured that ultimately they would conclude that "man, if I make my job easier, I could probably do things faster, and that means they'll put more work content into my fifty-seven seconds. So, I don't want any part of that." Since management presumed the attitudes of workers toward participation to be counterproductive, they did not expect valuable input from workers and had a system for reviewing submissions that the process control manager described as "quite a bureaucracy." "It's pretty impressive," he added sarcastically.

Focused Input in Arlington

If employee participation was widely embraced in Silao and marred by skepticism in Janesville, once again in Arlington we see an aspect of the GMS partially implemented, in this case with a focus on money. Both the directors of personnel and labor relations in Arlington reported widespread participation, with over 90 percent of their workforce submitting at least one recommendation per year. They further claimed that their plant ranked among GM's top facilities in terms of bonuses paid, with $400,000 having been distributed to workers the previous year. Though submissions made by workers were not displayed as predominately as in Silao, the plant maintained a thick binder containing a list of all the recommendations that had been submitted and whether they were accepted or not, alphabetized by workers' last names, so that anyone could check on their own or a coworker's history of participation.

Several workers indicated that they thought the 90 percent figure was artificially high, explaining that if a work group made up of a collection of teams had a 100 percent participation rate, management bought them pizza. So the groups would make sure everyone had signed onto at least one recommendation, many of which were "boneheaded ideas" according to a recent retiree who had worked on the assembly line and as a supervisor during his career. He estimated the real participation rate at 60 to 85 percent, which was still far higher than in Janesville.

Workers in Arlington submitted recommendation forms in boxes located throughout the plant. These were forwarded to a team of evaluators who would measure the impact of the proposal and either accept or reject the idea. What distinguished the participation program in Arlington was the emphasis on money in driving the system. Union officials and workers interviewed indicated management was responsive to ideas because they were always looking for ways to save money. The human resource manager concurred that they were interested in implementing workers' ideas "if it makes business sense." Workers were primarily interested in the bonuses. So an informal consensus formed that the system would focus on cost-saving ideas.

Even with the focus on cost-saving ideas, managers and union officials in Arlington reported that recommendations from workers peaked with the annual model-year changes that required all the footprints to be redrawn. So as in Silao, participation from line operators was a tool that helped management fine-tune the standardized routines at the heart of the GMS.

Standardized Work as the Heart of Lean Production

The comparison of the organization of work in Silao, Arlington, and Janesville identifies the strict standardization of work as the only common element of the GMS among the plants. This ability of the automaker to synchronize tasks to keep workers in near constant motion, with a stated benchmark of extracting fifty-five seconds of labor for each minute worked, has resulted in an intensification of work from the mass production era. Furthermore, in Silao and Arlington, where teamwork, Andon systems, and policies for garnering workers' ideas to improve their workplace were practiced, nobody in management or labor suggested they enhanced the quality of work through intellectual engagement with the manufacturing process. Rather, these components of the GMS were themselves highly standardized and functioned primarily to support the meticulous standardization of work considered crucial to the efficiency of the manufacturing system.

But how big a contribution do teamwork and employee participation make to productivity and quality? Lean proponents (Kenney and Florida 1993; Womack, Jones, and Roos 1990) assert there is a competitive imperative behind the reorganization of workers into teams that become involved in, and responsible for, improving product quality and productivity. If so, the plant in Silao should have outperformed the two U.S. plants.

Instead, the three plants performed comparably. According to J. D. Power & Associates, which produces an annual report on product quality that is the automotive industry standard, consumers of vehicles assembled in Janesville, Silao, and Arlington reported nearly identical rates of quality defects in the first three months of ownership. In its 2005 analysis, J. D. Power reported that purchasers of the SUVs reported 108 problems per 100 vehicles assembled in Janesville, and 109 problems per 100 vehicles made in Silao and Arlington (*Janesville Gazette*, May 29, 2005). Therefore, the overall quality of these large SUVs appeared not to be influenced by teamwork, the use of Andon systems, or the extent to which workers participated in *kaizen* activities.

Comparing productivity between the plants is a little more complicated. Productivity in the auto industry is conventionally measured in hours per vehicle (HPV)—how many labor hours are required to assemble one vehicle. When workers in Janesville complained that supervisors were obsessed with the numbers, they were frequently referring specifically to HPV. The lower the HPV, the higher the productivity. Unfortunately, direct comparisons of HPV among assembly plants can be misleading. Most fundamentally, more complex vehicles will be associated with higher HPV. A full-sized SUV will be associated with higher HPV than a small economy car. But even at factories producing similar vehicles such as in this study, different combinations of body styles and chassis configurations, levels of automation, and the degree to which components are outsourced rather than assembled in-house can all affect HPV in ways that have nothing to do with actual labor productivity.

To overcome this problem, I compare the rates of improvement in productivity from year to year to determine whether the version of the GMS in Silao was outperforming those in Janesville and Arlington. If teamwork and fully functioning Andon systems and employee participation programs are fundamental to productivity gains under lean production, the plant in Silao should have reported decreasing HPV at a faster rate than the plant in Arlington, which should have been outperforming the factory in Janesville.

This was not the case. Figure 2.1 graphs the HPV at each of the three plants from 1998 to 2004 (*Harbour Report North America*, 1999–2005), the years all three plants were assembling full-sized SUVs at full capacity. (Significant downtime was experienced in 2005 as the plants retooled to build the next generation of SUVs, followed by drops in demand for SUVs

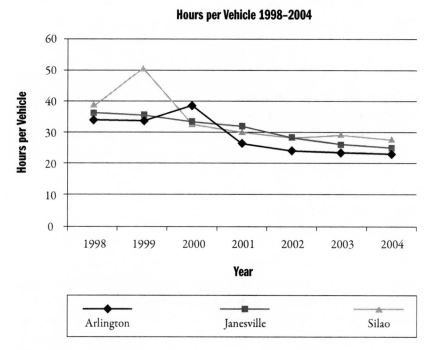

FIGURE 2.1 Productivity over time in hours per vehicle (*Source: The Harbour Report,* 1999–2005.)

that affected production in the ensuing years.) Each of the plants reported substantial improvements in their HPV. Arlington improved its productivity 38 percent over the period, from 33.78 to 22.39 HPV. Janesville cut its HPV 33 percent, from 36.17 to 24.28. Silao improved 29 percent, cutting HPV from 38.13 to 27.02. Both Silao and Arlington had years when their productivity declined sharply due to the launch of new vehicles (represented as a spike on the graph), which is typical until the assembly line is ratcheted up to full speed. In Silao, this was exacerbated by a shortage of parts (*Harbour Report North America* 2000). The launch of the Cadillac Escalade, Chevy Tahoe, and GMC Yukon in Arlington in 2000 was accompanied by the installation of a new automated body shop, which most likely accounts for the sudden dip in HPV from 33.36 to 25.99 between 1999 and 2001.

Once all three plants had stabilized their production, between 2001 through 2004 they each demonstrated consistent productivity growth. In fact, over the period, productivity gains at the Janesville plant outpaced the other two plants, maintaining a persistent decline since 1998 even though, as this research demonstrates and *Harbour Reports* indicates, the plant was "behind most GM plants on the GMS journey" (*Habour Report* 2004, 193). But by successfully standardizing work and increasing the workload of each line operator, Janesville kept pace with both the Silao and Arlington plants in terms of productivity. These findings lend further support to studies challenging the idea that productivity necessarily improves with teamwork and employee participation schemes (Cappelli and Neumark 2001; Godard 2004; Ichniowski, Shaw, and Prennushi 1997), and reaffirms the centrality of standardized work to the lean production assembly line.

Rethinking the Reorganization of Work in the Auto Industry

Why did lean production intensify work without providing the intellectual challenge proponents hoped, and why does teamwork and participation seem to matter so little to plant performance? Answers to these questions lie, in part, in the framing of the differences between the lean and mass production paradigms. In particular, in emphasizing the advent of teamwork and participation schemes under lean production, scholars often caricatured work along the mass production assembly line as fulfilling

Taylor's (1911) call for the separation of the conception and execution of work (Vidal 2007), where "workers struggle to assemble" what Womack, Jones, and Roos consider to be "unmanufacturable products and have no way to improve their working environment" (Womack, Jones, and Roos 1990, 101–2). But automobiles were being assembled by workers who had to problem solve on an ad-hoc basis, often with their coworkers, precisely because the parts they were installing were designed and manufactured with far less precision than they are today. Taking such initiative required intellectual engagement (and sometimes a rubber mallet). In fact, workers in Janesville and Arlington who had experienced the shift from mass to lean production sometimes expressed feeling less intellectually engaged under the GMS.

Toyota's innovation may not have been in reengaging workers' intellects, but in formalizing teamwork and the appropriation by the firm of the know-how that under mass production workers possessed as their own tricks of the trade. This allowed Toyota to systematically root out and address the causes of problems so that the assembly process became more productive with improved quality. In their rereading of his work, Crowley et al. (2010) suggest that this is exactly what Taylor prescribed, and not the total disregard for workers' knowledge that has been attributed to him. If so, the transition from mass to lean production on the assembly line is a turn toward Taylorism, not away from it.

Logically, as this "neo-Taylorist" (Crowley et al. 2010) system eliminates imperfections in the production process, the capacity to standardize work and keep workers moving increases, while the need and opportunity for workers to problem solve on the assembly line decreases. Factor in technological advances in the design of automobiles, their parts, and the assembly lines on which they are made, and work becomes ever increasingly routinized and less cerebral, as its pace intensifies. It may very well be that in the era when Toyota developed lean production, formalizing teams of workers with the capacity to stop the assembly line and help reorganize work garnered significant efficiencies for the firm. Decades later, the design of automobiles and their parts may have now become sufficiently sophisticated that workers' ideas and contributions are of decreasing marginal import. As a result, it may make little difference whether the process of eliminating defects in production is carried out exclusively by industrial engineers without workers' input, as in Janesville, or through widespread employee participation, as in Silao.

Teamwork, job rotation, and *kaizen* activities did appear to bring some relief to the standardized routines that dominated the workday, especially if workers rotated off the line to perform administrative tasks as they did in Silao. In fact, having already been subjected to the intensification of work along the assembly line, workers in Janesville and Arlington would have benefited from a more thorough implementation of the other elements of lean production implemented in Silao. However, it is highly unlikely that GM would have been willing to absorb the labor costs associated with rotating workers in their U.S. plants off the assembly line for a portion of each day. Neither is it the case that the UAW at either the national or local levels were clamoring for a more authentic lean production system that might spell their members from the labor of the assembly line for a small portion of the day. The union understood that doing so risked compromising a plant's competitiveness, and that workers might perceive such an embrace of lean production as a further concession to management.

Regardless, the notion that "Taylorism is pretty much dead in our society" (Barone 2008) is misguided. Lean production has certainly revolutionized the auto industry, and in many areas of automotive production, from design to supply chain management, it represents a paradigm shift away from Fordist mass production. But mass production was never pure Taylorism, and work under lean production incorporates Taylor's ideas for standardized labor. Workers may have been reorganized into teams. They may have been given Andon cords and opportunities to contribute their ideas. But in Silao and Arlington these were implemented to reinforce the primacy of standardized work. As a result, as the North American auto industry globalized, assembly-line workers have not been liberated from the drudgery of mass production to enjoy greater satisfaction at work. Rather, job quality has declined as work has become increasingly routinized and its pace intensified. The processes by which globalization resulted in an intensification of work in an industry that was once characterized by high levels of union control over the shop floor, and the reasons behind the differences in implementation of the GMS in the three plants, is explained in the ensuing chapters.

3

Whipsawed!

Local Unions Fight for
Jobs in the United States

In November 2008, with GM seeking a federal loan to stave off bankruptcy, UAW president Ron Gettlelfinger assured the Senate Banking Committee that "union-negotiated work rules cannot be blamed for the current problems facing the Detroit-based companies. According to the *Harbour Report*, the industry benchmark for productivity, union-represented workers are actually more efficient than their counterparts at non-union auto plants. And union-made vehicles built by the Detroit-based auto companies are winning quality awards from *Consumer Reports*, J. D. Power, and other industry analysts." Although Gettelfinger's testimony was met with some skepticism on Capitol Hill, the previous chapter substantiates his claims. The strict standardization of work at the heart of the lean production process was successfully implemented in Janesville and Arlington, allowing those facilities to operate as efficiently as the plant in Silao, where the union had no presence on the shop floor.

Left unsaid by Gettelfinger in his testimony was that in matching the productivity of nonunion auto plants, the implementation of lean production had intensified the pace of work on the assembly line. But the UAW president was not in Washington to warn of declining working conditions. He was there to cheerlead labor-management cooperation and the rising productivity through which the Detroit automakers could once again become profitable—if Congress would agree to lend them money to stave off bankruptcy. (Congress declined and the Bush and Obama administrations used funds from the Troubled Asset Relief Program to save GM and Chrysler.) But how, and why, did the president of the UAW become a champion of rising labor productivity instead of improved working conditions?

Clearly, Gettelfinger's testimony was tailored to the immediate crisis and the need to save the Detroit automakers. However, his embrace of lean production and cooperative labor relations, even in the face of intensified work on the assembly line, was not new within the UAW. As far back as the 1980s, local UAW leaders in places such as Janesville and Arlington began publicly embracing lean production, espousing the benefits of cooperation with management, and highlighting improved productivity and quality. And just as Gettelfinger hoped that his testimony before Congress would keep auto plants open and save jobs across the United States, local union leaders supported efforts to implement lean production to keep their plants open and save their members' jobs.

Beginning in the 1980s, the Detroit automakers' declining market share led them to close auto plants to reduce excess capacity. At the same time, they were attempting to implement lean production, and the willingness of a workforce to embrace lean production became a factor in decisions over which facilities to keep operating and which to shutter. What ensued was a competition between local workforces and their unions to curry favor with the automakers by conceding workplace rights and local labor standards. The winners kept their jobs. The losers saw their plant close, with much of the workforce packing up and relocating to surviving facilities in an effort to hold on to a good job.

This whipsawing, as the Detroit automakers' strategy of pitting local factories and their unions against one another became known, required more of local unions than mere concessions in the "union-negotiated work rules" to which Gettelfinger referred. Local union leaders had to talk the talk, advocating to their own members the benefits of lean production, cooperation with management, and rising productivity. Through whipsawing, the very character of labor relations between the Detroit automakers and the UAW transitioned from hegemonic control to hegemonic despotism. Under hegemonic control, labor was *"granted* concessions on the basis of the expansion of profits" and, in return, maintained the discipline necessary to carry out production. Under hegemonic despotism, labor *"makes* concessions on the basis of the relative profitability" (Burawoy 1985, 150; italics in the original) of the industry, giving up what it once won at the bargaining table in order to keep its employers competitive.

In gaining concessions allowing them to reorganize work, the Detroit automakers exploited the bifurcated nature of auto industry collective bargaining. Wages and benefits are negotiated nationally, and the dynamic by which the automakers extracted concessions from the UAW in these areas is explained in chapter 5. Work rules and plant governance, on the other hand, are negotiated between local management and union leaders at individual factories. These local labor contracts have traditionally included job descriptions, the plant seniority system by which jobs are assigned or chosen, safety and health standards, and any other issues concerning conditions of work, which might include everything from payment schedules to establishing cleanliness standards for the bathrooms, employee entitlement to lockers, and parking regulations at the plant (Tolliday and Zeitlin 1992). As I was repeatedly reminded by GM management and union officials in Janesville and Arlington, local labor agreements have always asserted a managerial right to organize production. But management's discretion is qualified by the rights and obligations of local unions to protect their members' safety and health and ensure decent working conditions. Labor's rights under these contracts are enforced by union representatives within the plants.

This chapter recounts the process by which GM whipsawed local unions and workers in Janesville and Arlington to illustrate the manner in which Detroit automakers manufactured consent (Burawoy 1979) for the intensification of work along the assembly line as the globalization of the industry brought competition from nonunion transplants owned by foreign automakers. The chapter also provides insight into the way factory history and future prospects help shape the specific organization of work on the shop floor described in chapter 2. In both Janesville and Arlington, the plants had segued from mass production to lean production, and were ultimately implementing their respective versions of the GMS. Yet the degree to which each factory embraced teamwork and employee participation reflected its historical context. In Janesville, those elements had been at one time embraced, only to be suddenly abandoned by management. That experience, and expectations that the plant's days were numbered, left little foundation on which to rebuild those programs. The prospect of long-term production in Arlington, however, provided sufficient incentives for management and labor in that plant to adopt elements of teamwork and employee participation important to the GMS.

In both these plants, lean production was implemented where mass production was once the norm, and workers' experiences of globalization included the transition from one manufacturing system to the other. So the chapter begins by recounting the growth in production and evolution of labor relations in Janesville and Arlington during the mass production era. This history sets the stage for describing the effect of whipsawing on workers and their local unions as GM's fortunes shifted and the automaker began closing factories. The chapter concludes by accounting for the variation in the GMS at the two plants due to their divergent histories and prospects for the future. Much of the chapter focuses on the period from the mid-1980s to the early 1990s, which in both Janesville and Arlington proved seminal in shaping the factory regimes of the early twenty-first century.

Automotive Expansion in Janesville and Arlington

Until the factory closed at the end of 2008, the history of auto assembly in Janesville closely followed the trajectory of GM and the U.S. auto industry overall. Automobile production began in Janesville in 1923 in a factory that originally built Samson Tractors. GM had purchased Samson Tractor a few years earlier, but lack of competitiveness and safety concerns over its rein-steered model caused them to cease production. In 1923, GM employed 660 of Janesville's 18,000 residents, who produced 42,509 cars and trucks that year. By 1929, according to the local *Janesville Gazette*, the plant and its 2,500 workers produced their 500,000th automobile, one of over 124,000 vehicles that rolled off the assembly line that year. The plant housed two assembly lines belonging to two different divisions of GM. The bodies of the cars were manufactured by GM's Fisher Body division. Those bodies were then attached to the chassis in the Chevrolet portion of the plant, which had a daily quota of 610 vehicles (*Janesville Gazette*, June 14, 1973).

Even as GM's divisions changed, the Janesville facility would operate two separate assembly lines for most of its lifetime.

During the Great Depression, production in Janesville declined until GM shut the plant in September 1932, citing excessive state income taxes and fears that Wisconsin would soon institute an unemployment tax. A year later, the automaker announced that it would reopen the plant after the culmination of the Chicago World's Fair, where GM's exhibition featured roughly two hundred former Janesville employees building cars on a model assembly line (*Janesville Gazette*, September 21, 1983). The decision to restart production was celebrated with a "Janesville Jubilee Day," which the *Janesville Gazette* reported included a parade, a banquet attended by the governor, and a free dance featuring "old time and modern music."

With the U.S. entry into World War II, the Janesville facility was converted to wartime production, manufacturing artillery shells and parts for army and navy vehicles. Once the war ended, production of trucks and full-size automobiles resumed, and over the next forty years the plant grew in both physical size and importance to the local economy. By the early 1970s the factory had grown from its original 321,000 square feet to cover 2.3 million square feet. A second shift was added in the early 1950s (*Janesville Gazette*, September 21, 1983) as production increased from a little over 100,000 vehicles in 1947 to more than 316,000 by 1965 (*Janesville Gazette*, June 14, 1973). By 1981, the plant employed roughly six thousand production workers on two assembly lines, one assembling the Chevy Caprice and Impala, and the other pickup trucks. At the time, GM employed more than one-third of the Janesville area workforce (*Janesville Gazette*, September 21, 1983).

If the Janesville plant followed the long trajectory of GM's rise, the factory in Arlington, Texas, reflected the automaker's postwar expansion. In 1952, GM broke ground on the new factory in Arlington, at the time a four-square-mile farming town of 7,800 residents nestled between the cities of Dallas and Fort Worth (*New York Times*, January 12, 1992). In the wake of World War II, the plant was designed with a sufficiently high roof to accommodate the manufacture of airplanes, just in case GM would again have to switch to wartime production. Although that never occurred, in the lean production era of automation and just-in-time delivery, the overhead space became occupied by some of the eighteen miles of conveyors that local management said delivered sequenced parts to the assembly line, reducing the number of off-line material handling jobs that workers with high seniority cherished.

Auto assembly commenced in 1954, with a single shift of 366 hourly workers building the Pontiac Chieftain. By the end of the year, employment exceeded 1,800, and in 1955 the Arlington plant produced more than 110,000 cars. As in Janesville, production and employment grew for the next three decades. By 1985, when the plant's 4,400 workers (*Arlington Daily News*, March 5, 1986) rolled its five-millionth car off the assembly line, the factory had built an assortment of Pontiac, Chevrolet, Oldsmobile, and Buick passenger cars (*Arlington News*, February 27, 1992). And even as the city of Arlington grew to ninety-six square miles, with its own professional baseball team, and a population that exceeded a quarter million, GM remained a major employer and taxpayer (*New York Times*, January 12, 1992).

The Rise of Local Unions and Hegemonic Control

Just as the history of the Janesville factory followed the evolution of the auto industry as a whole, so, too, labor relations at the plant hewed closely to developments in the industry. According to the history of Local 95 prepared for its fiftieth anniversary in 1985, (*UAW 50 Years* 1985), the union in Janesville was founded in 1933 by eight men meeting secretly at a corner gas station, a couple of years before the passage of the National Labor Relations Act (NLRA) would legally protect workers from being fired for attempting to organize a union. Four years later, workers in Janesville participated in the 1937 sit-down strike through which the UAW gained recognition by General Motors. Unlike the more well-known Flint sit-down strikers, however, local union activists in Janesville reached an agreement with factory managers to vacate the plant after only nine hours on the condition that management not operate the facility until the industrial dispute in Flint was settled (*Janesville Gazette*, January 5, 1937). With the resolution of the strike six weeks later (*Janesville Gazette*, February 16, 1937), workers in Janesville became members of the United Auto Workers Locals 95 and 121 in the Fisher Body and Chevrolet portions of the plant, respectively. Local 121 merged into Local 95 in 1968, when a reorganization at GM folded both Fisher Body and Chevrolet into the General Motors Assembly Division, creating a single employer at the Janesville facility (*UAW 50 Years*

1985). Local 95 grew into an amalgamated union representing workers in sixteen businesses in the Janesville area by 2005, including several local suppliers to GM.

Establishing the local union in Arlington was far less eventful than in Janesville. By the 1950s, the UAW was well established and a national process for gaining union representation had become firmly established. Instead of occupying their factory to force recognition of their union by GM, workers in Arlington simply voted. Within a month after the plant began production, representatives from the UAW began an organizing campaign by handing out leaflets at the factory gate. In February 1954, a vote was held in which workers voted 804 to 21 in favor of affiliation with the UAW. Local 276 received its charter from the UAW on March 11, and four days later the workers became covered by the UAW's national collective bargaining agreement with GM. Like Local 95 in Janesville, Local 276 eventually grew into an amalgamated union that represented workers at a number of facilities, including some of GM's local suppliers.

Within the assembly plants in Janesville and Arlington, the basic structures and functions of the two local unions was similar, and remained steady over the years, though the specific number of union representatives changed. Both Local 95 and 276 had a president and an executive board elected to run the local union. Within GM's assembly plants, the workers were represented by a Bargaining Committee led by a shop chairperson who held ultimate responsibility for negotiating and enforcing the local collective bargaining agreement. In Janesville, the shop chairperson was assisted by zone committeepersons representing different areas of the plant, who also oversaw district committeepersons who served as the first line of union representation for workers on the shop floor. The union bureaucracy in Arlington functioned similarly, but was a little flatter, with district committeepersons reporting directly to the shop chair. At both plants, as at all the UAW local unions representing GM's employees throughout the United States, all union officials were elected for three-year terms during which they remained on GM's payroll, though they worked full-time representing the workers and performed no production work.

Among their most important duties, district committeepersons represented workers who wished to contest treatment by supervisors. In fact, the first step in the grievance procedure as outlined in the national collective bargaining agreement was for a committeeperson to resolve a dispute with a worker's foreman. (Though the rise of women into union leadership roles had caused official titles to become gender neutral, workers with whom I spoke more typically referred to their "committeeman" or "zoneman"—even if that person was a woman.) This provided workers along the assembly line a representative armed with a contract detailing workers' rights and obligations to defend them against a supervisor. And in most cases, this was sufficient to handle problems that arose.

If not, unresolved grievances could work their way up the union and management hierarchies. First they would be written up for discussion at weekly meetings between union representatives and the plant superintendent. If still unresolved, a representative from the UAW headquarters would join the shop chair in taking up the issue with the plant manager and personnel director. Eventually, grievances over important or contentious issues could be addressed by GM and the UAW leadership in national negotiations.

The structure of the local union bureaucracies and the formal grievance procedure complemented the factories' strictly defined job classifications typical of the mass production era. In 1947, workers in the Fisher Body side of the Janesville plant alone were divided into nearly two hundred job classifications, so narrowly defined that thirty-five of them applied only to a single worker. Each job classification was associated with a separate wage rate, ranging from sixty cents an hour for women sewing seats on the "cushion line" (the only part of the plant where women could work until the 1970s) to $1.05 an hour for a few of the jobs in the paint department (*UAW 50 Years* 1985). By the mid-1980s, as work became less specialized and increasingly automated, the number of job classifications had declined to ninety (*Janesville Gazette*, February 13, 1987). Similarly, in Arlington, workers were initially divided into 120 job classifications.

In addition to job classifications, local labor contracts grew to cover almost every aspect of plant operation. The detailed nature of the local collective bargaining agreements provided local unions ample ammunition to file grievances, and the formal grievance procedure developed into both a system for resolving disputes and an avenue by which the union could exercise power and control over the shop floor, in spite of management's contractual right to organize production. Supervisors and foremen knew that the union could damage their performance in the eyes of senior management by making them the subject of numerous grievances. If relations with management were good, technical violations of the contract could be overlooked. If relations were tense, written grievances could be produced in vast numbers, legitimate or not, just to overwhelm management with paperwork. In this way, grievances became bargaining chips at the local level and also during negotiations over the national agreements. In fact, the willingness of UAW representatives in national negotiations to bargain away grievances over work rules sometimes caused conflict with local unions looking for resolution of those issues (Katz 1985).

Competition, Contraction, and the Rise of Despotic Hegemony

The relative control that local unions enjoyed over factory operations was premised on the growth and profitability of GM. As long as the company was expanding, it needed to maintain production and could afford to pay the price to keep workers satisfied. But as increased competition left the Detroit automakers with overcapacity and a competitive urgency to begin implementing lean production, this dynamic reversed. In a shift to hegemonic despotism (Burawoy 1985), the automakers began threatening plant closure unless they were granted concessions from local unions and the assistance of local union leadership in driving productivity gains.[1]

Through whipsawing, the automakers pitted plant against plant in an implicit, and at times explicit, high-stakes competition for jobs that reached well outside the factory gates. Just as foreign automakers encouraged local and state governments to offer tax incentives, fund training programs, and make infrastructure improvements to lure new transplants to their regions, the Detroit automakers began entertaining such offers as they considered which plants to keep and which to close (Barlett and Steele 1998).[1]

Within the factories, local management, whose own jobs were threatened by a potential plant closure, sought changes to local collective bargaining agreements that would facilitate the intensification of work and cost cutting necessary to become lean. Job classifications were consolidated and seniority systems altered to give management more flexibility over their use of labor. Line operators were organized into teams with team leaders that performed duties once reserved for supervisors, thereby facilitating the elimination of scores of middle managers. Work hours were altered to cut overhead. In some cases, the local unions began allowing the automakers to contract out certain services, from custodial duties to elements of material handling, in order to save money and cut hours per vehicle.

The concessions sought, however, were in rhetorical tone as well as contract content. Even as the automakers broke labor solidarity between plants and sought concessions to work rules and local standards, they simultaneously demanded union leaders adopt the language of teamwork and cooperation. So in urging their members to ratify the new agreements, local union leadership had to sell concessions in workplace rights and work rules as a new era of labor-management cooperation that would prove less stressful and potentially offer more gratifying work, just as proponents of lean production claim. No doubt, some local union leaders believed in the possibility of labor-management cooperation, and hoped the new manufacturing systems really were built upon the promise of greater respect for workers. Others had no such illusions. They were just trying to save their factories and the jobs of their members.

Documenting whipsawing can be difficult. The automakers deny engaging in it. Local union leaders deny succumbing to it, as part of their obligation to maintain the façade of cooperative labor relations, but also to win reelection. Weakness is not a selling point in a union election. Still, the factory histories in Janesville and Arlington reveal the tactics and process of whipsawing through which GM not only took back control of the shop floors but also enlisted the local unions in the drive to intensify work.

Seeds of Change in Janesville

In Janesville, as throughout the U.S. auto industry, the oil crises and recessions of the 1970s brought layoffs and set the stage for the introduction of the Japanese automobiles that would radically alter the way the industry operated. In 1974, GM's sales declined 27 percent from the previous year (*Janesville Gazette*, January 7, 1975). By the end of the year 240,000 of the nation's 690,000 autoworkers were out of work, including 63,000 of GM's employees (*Janesville Gazette*, December 19, 1974). At the end of 1974, after a series of short layoffs in Janesville (*Janesville Gazette*, December 29, 1973; January 25, 1974; March 8, 1974), GM idled the entire second shift, laying off 2,100 workers for seven months (*Janesville Gazette*, November 29, 1974; April 24, 1975).

Once that recession ended, and gas prices dropped, sales rebounded. In the third quarter of 1977, GM became the first U.S. industrial firm to record more than a billion dollars in profit in one quarter (*Janesville Gazette*, July 28, 1977). In Janesville, the plant returned to full capacity, with nearly six thousand workers producing 252,000 Chevy Caprices and Impalas and more than 118,000 pickup trucks in 1978 (*Janesville Gazette*, January 26, 1979).

Yet it was not to last. The oil crisis that began in 1979 ushered in more permanent change. As GM's sales during the first quarter of 1980 fell to their lowest point since 1975 (*Janesville Gazette*, April 24, 1980), including an especially sharp drop in sales of the automaker's largest vehicles assembled in Janesville, layoffs struck again. As in the previous recession, these began as a series of short layoffs to adjust inventory levels (*Janesville Gazette*, March 4, 1980; April 16, 1980; May 5, 1980; June 5, 1980). And as in the previous recession, by the end of 1980 the entire second shift of both the auto and pickup truck assembly lines had been laid off for months (*Janesville Gazette*, November 4, 1980). For much of the year, half the Janesville workforce was among the nearly three hundred thousand autoworkers laid off across the country (*Janesville Gazette*, June 6, 1980).

By the end of the recession, the globalization of the North American auto industry was under way. The 1980s marked a turning point of steadily declining market share for the Detroit automakers as first Japanese, and later European and Korean, automakers gained a foothold in the U.S. market. As GM scrambled to compete with the smaller automobiles produced by Japanese automakers, the Janesville plant was shut down for seven months to enlarge and update the facility to build small, four-cylinder, front-wheel-drive cars (*Janesville Gazette*, July 28, 1980). Over fifty robots were added to the body shop, which according to GM officials made the Janesville facility among the most "automated and flexible vehicle assembly facilities" (*Janesville Gazette*, June 1, 1982) in the world. Theoretically, this would help close the productivity gap enjoyed by Japanese automakers. The Janesville plant manager confidently reported that "we will have one of the most modern, efficient automobile assembly plants in the industry and will want to keep it operating at the highest capacity as possible" (*Janesville Gazette*, July 28, 1980).

Such predictions proved overly optimistic. In June 1982 workers in Janesville began producing the Chevy Cavalier and its more expensive cousin, the Cadillac Cimarron. But sales lagged to only one-third of GM's initial expectations (*Janesville Gazette*, November 26, 1982), requiring only one shift of workers to fill demand. The eighteen hundred workers on the second shift were not called back until June 1983, twenty months after they were originally laid off for the retooling (*Janesville Gazette*, June 4, 1983).

Perhaps as a reflection of concern for job security, workers in Janesville voted in far greater numbers than autoworkers elsewhere to accept concessions to the national labor agreement negotiated between GM and the UAW in the beginning of 1982. The renegotiated collective bargaining agreement saved GM $2.5 billion by deferring cost-of-living adjustments (COLAs) for June, September, and December 1982, freezing wages for the thirty-month life of contract, and forcing workers to forfeit nine paid holidays per year. In exchange, GM agreed to a temporary moratorium on plant closings. With nearly half of GM's 320,000 line workers laid off (*Janesville Gazette*, March 22, 1982), the contract was approved with 54 percent of the vote nationwide (*Janesville Gazette*, April 9, 1982), a far lower margin than in Janesville, where 77 percent voted in favor of ratification (*Janesville Gazette*, April 5, 1982).

In fact, in Janesville the ensuing two decades were marked by uncertainty, with the local union, community, and state fighting to keep the plant operating, under persistent whipsawing and pressure to increase productivity. By the middle of 2002, the plant was down to one assembly line and 3,600 hourly workers, more than two thousand less than at its peak. The local collective bargaining agreement had been rewritten to facilitate the intensification of work. The local union had first become an advocate of lean production and later the reluctant enforcer of the GMS. Several distinct episodes helped bring about this change.

Fort Wayne and the Goddamned '86ers

Local 95 in Janesville was among the first unions to experience and succumb to whipsawing by GM. Even as auto sales picked up, and employment in Janesville reached 5,800 line operators in 1983 (*Janesville Gazette*, September 3, 1983), concern for jobs remained. Janesville was scheduled to continue building pickup trucks only through the 1986 model year, and in August 1984 the company announced that it was consolidating its assembly of light duty trucks at a new $600 million factory in Fort Wayne, Indiana (*Janesville Gazette*, August 31, 1984). Fearful for their jobs, a little over twelve hundred workers transferred from Janesville to open the new factory in Fort Wayne (*Janesville Gazette*, March 1, 1984). Recalling his decision to move to Indiana, from where he eventually returned, the shop chair in Janesville said, "My dad was union president at the time. He said, 'I'm not gonna tell you what to do, but if you want to retire from General Motors, you probably have a better chance down there than up here.'"

The line operators who departed for Fort Wayne were soon replaced by "temporary" workers in Janesville, ostensibly hired to work for the short period it would take GM to shift assembly of the pickup trucks from Janesville to Fort Wayne. According to one worker hired in 1986, they were all told, "Don't buy a car. Don't buy a house. This is temporary."

Temporary it was not. Desperate to save jobs, and in response to warnings by plant management that, as reported in the local *Janesville Gazette*, "several GM plants, the Japanese, and other competitors have improved faster than we have," and that "other parts of the country and world want our jobs" (*Janesville Gazette*, May 9, 1986), Local 95 began renegotiating its labor contract with local management. In September 1986, an agreement was reached that granted management greater flexibility by slashing the number of job classifications from ninety to only three; the agreement also saved GM overhead by converting the forty-hour work week from five, eight-hour-days to four, ten-hour-days on a trial basis (*Janesville Gazette*, September 22, 1986).

Having successfully extracted concessions from Local 95, GM announced the following month that Janesville would not be among the eleven plants the company was looking to close (*Janesville Gazette*, October 29, 1986). Instead, GM assigned the assembly of crew-cab pickups to Janesville (*Janesville Gazette*, November 6, 1986), extending the life of that assembly line until 1989 and saving 1,100 jobs—nearly enough jobs for all the workers who had agreed to transfer to Fort Wayne. Yet even those who had not yet moved were not permitted to rescind their decision to go (*Janesville Gazette*, March 1, 1986).

The following February, after GM chairman Roger Smith complimented the Janesville plant for its "super attention to detail and quality and an understanding and cooperative relationship" (*Janesville Gazette*, January 8, 1987), the automaker announced it would move assembly of medium-duty trucks to Janesville from Pontiac, Michigan (*Janesville Gazette*, February 12, 1987), where UAW Local 594 had refused to rework their collective bargaining agreement along the same lines that Local 95 had the previous year (*Janesville Gazette*, January 3, 1987). Janesville workers then voted to make the four day, forty-hour-week permanent (*Janesville Gazette*, May 29, 1987).

In the course of a year, GM had uprooted 1,200 workers who moved to Indiana and replaced them with fresh hires who would forever be known in Janesville as the "(goddamned) '86ers." Similar to workers in Silao who had landed the best jobs in the area, those 1,200 new workers in the Janesville plant would consider themselves lucky as their temporary jobs became permanent. Without any experience with the previous organization of work or its associated labor relations, '86ers were hired under a new collective bargaining agreement with the reduced job classifications, greater flexibility for management, and cost savings that GM wanted. Nearly twenty years later, workers in Janesville who remembered the episode were convinced that it was, in the words of one union zone committeeperson, a case of "corporate manipulation." Likewise, the president of Local 95 contended it "was all by design." As a result, the uprooting of those Janesville workers became a lasting symbol of manipulation by the automaker. However, it was only the first whipsawing that workers in Janesville would experience, and through which GM would reassert control over the shop floor.

An Experiment in "Jointness"

Though they had won a temporary reprieve from plant closure in 1987, Local 95 and its members were vulnerable to further concessions because the Janesville facility still lacked a product to build long-term. The assembly line on which medium-duty trucks were assembled was relatively short, requiring less than a thousand workers. The plant was winding down assembly of the pickup trucks that would be assembled at GM's new plant in Fort Wayne. The version of the Chevy Cavalier they were building was only scheduled for production into 1991. Survival of the plant depended, therefore, on a decision by GM over the following few years to invest in retooling to assemble a new product.

Of course, by the mid-1980s, GM was trying to catch up to the Japanese automakers that had gained a foothold in the U.S. market by offering consumers a choice of small, fuel-efficient cars that had earned a reputation for superior quality. Though several years before the publication of *The Machine That Changed the World* (Womack, Jones, and Roos 1990) would popularize the term "lean production," the success of automakers such as Toyota was already being attributed, in part, to a spirit of labor-management cooperation that nourished teamwork, empowered workers to identify imperfections in production and, if need be, to halt the assembly line so that defects could be addressed at their source.

To remain competitive, GM would need to somehow cultivate sufficient labor-management cooperation and communication to build in-station. The automaker labeled this effort to simultaneously reorganize work and transform labor relations "Jointness." GM encouraged plant managers and local unions to embrace Jointness as a matter of survival. As the automaker was deciding which of its factories to shut to reduce overcapacity, friendly labor relations were among the factors on which the factories were being judged. Local management and union leaders had to demonstrate to corporate headquarters that they could work collaboratively, rather than as adversaries, to improve both productivity and quality.

In Janesville, implementation of Jointness began in 1986, in an effort to get a replacement for the assembly line producing pickup trucks that was moving to Fort Wayne, and with an eye toward ensuring production beyond 1991. As the president of Local 95 told a reporter, he was "concerned about operating in 1990. Can we compete and make cars in 1990 and make these jobs secure?" The union's shop chair concurred, but also suggested that he had bought into the idea that labor relations on the shop floor could be improved and work made more satisfying. He indicated that renegotiating the local collective bargaining agreement was "an effort to save production on the truck line, but most assuredly to improve the quality of our jobs to help retain the car line because the car situation isn't that great." Working with the plant manager, the union leaders hoped to diffuse tensions between labor and management, improve productivity and product quality, and make the plant a better place to work. The shop chair explained that they were interconnected goals: "I don't think many people have really enjoyed their jobs here. What we're trying to get is so they can enjoy going to work, being given the proper respect and attention so they'll like the job, want to do it right and do it right the first time" (*Janesville Gazette*, August 28, 1986).

Over the next several years, even as Local 95 was accused by other local unions within the UAW of succumbing to whipsawing by conceding to management's demands (*Janesville Gazette*, April 16, 1987), the local union leadership continued to work with plant management to improve their relationship and those of workers and supervisors on the shop floor. Under the auspices of Jointness, work rules negotiated to protect line operators from arbitrary decisions by management were relaxed to allow for the implementation of the "team concept," even though the president of Local 95 indicated it was "a buzzword. If you asked anybody for a definition of it, they couldn't tell you" (*Janesville Gazette*, July 10, 1987). "Quality of Work Life" programs were instituted to address workers' concerns and complaints about their jobs, with two-day training sessions during which workers, their supervisors, and union representatives could, according to the plant manager at the time, "get to know each other and their jobs." Through a joint union-management "Discovery" program, workers were interviewed about every aspect of their jobs and how they could be improved. The "GM Quality Network" brought union representatives and local management together on a weekly basis "just to talk about business" and share "more and more information—previously sensitive information like cost" (*Janesville Gazette*, January 21, 1989), according to the plant manager. Two hourly workers joined management in assessing employees' suggestions, with details fed to the press of the financial awards paid to workers for their ideas (*Janesville Gazette*, April 26, 1988). The local *Janesville Gazette* ran at least nine such stories in 1988 alone, reporting that in the first year of the program workers were awarded over half a million dollars and the local plant set new quality records for itself (*Janesville Gazette*, June 27, 1988).

By early 1989, when GM was publicly ruminating over whether or not to move assembly of Chevy Suburbans from Flint, Michigan, to either Janesville or Leeds, Missouri, Local 95 had gained a reputation for working closely with management. A month before GM announced that Janesville would be awarded the product line, the workers in Flint renegotiated their local collective bargaining agreement to adopt provisions Local 95 had agreed to two and a half years earlier (*Janesville Gazette*, January 23, 1989). For their efforts, GM's president praised Flint's workers for having "displayed considerable foresight by adopting changes that will improve the plant's competitiveness" and suggested that he was "confident that Flint Assembly will meet the objectives recently approved in their local contract and that we will be able to jointly work with them on a new truck product that will be competitive in the tough truck marketplace" (*Janesville Gazette*, February 14, 1989). Nonetheless, the Chevy Suburban assembly line was moving to Janesville.

When the Janesville plant manager announced that Janesville would be assembling the SUV, he lauded the shop chairman for "working with us and [being] willing to look ahead and take a chance once in a while and do things that are good for the people, all of us." Otherwise, "we wouldn't be here today." For his part, the shop chairman claimed that he had once been the "most radical mother," always fighting hard against management, but that he had to change because "there are too many cars and trucks out there and too many plants. You can sit and bury your head and complain—or improve everything you can." Over time, he claimed to have become truly convinced, realizing that "it's unbelievable the power you have and what you can accomplish" working together with management. "You sit down with management and have an equal say. That doesn't mean you don't have fights," but the dynamic had changed. "Fifty years ago, management thought they were God. Union men got power by being tough and forceful." However, in Janesville, they were "trying to give the power to everybody. That scares some union people. You give the working people the proper process and support, and attitude and morale shoots way up" (*Janesville Gazette*, February 15, 1989).

Early Whipsawing in Arlington

As in Janesville, the latter half of the 1980s and the early 1990s were a turning point in Arlington. The reality of plant closings and GM's demand for more conciliatory labor relations hit in 1986, when workers were informed that their facility would not be among those selected to assemble GM's new product line of midsized, front-wheel-drive vehicles (*Arlington Daily News*, January 14, 1986). The previous year, Local 276 had declined to negotiate changes to their labor agreement similar to those being agreed to in Janesville. And though GM's director of media relations in Detroit insisted to the local *Arlington Daily News* that "it's not in the spirit of the CPC [Chevrolet-Pontiac-Canada] group to seek concessions from UAW employees or anyone else" (*Arlington Daily News*, January 15, 1986), he also indicated "that there has to be a cooperative attitude for any plant to be competitive. . . . Anything they do in Arlington to enhance labor relations makes them more competitive" (*Arlington Daily News*, February 26, 1986). GM's vice president and director of operations for the CPC

Group was more explicit in describing the failure of the Arlington plant to secure the new product line as a "learning experience" and "an experience in competition":

> Arlington has a future right now building the Monte Carlo and Cutlass. It has a challenge to produce them with higher quality and more efficiency than other facilities building similar models.... There can be life after the Monte Carlo and Cutlass.... The future is there for those who prepare for it. I'm confident the Arlington plant will be prepared to grab for the brass ring the next time it comes by.... We have to learn to cooperate, so a labor agreement is just the formal recognition of the way we do business, not an adversarial document. (*Arlington Daily News*, March 7, 1986)

In the face of such comments from GM's headquarters, local management positioned itself as in partnership with Local 276, calling rumors that some Monte Carlo production might be done in Pontiac, Michigan, "just speculation at this point," but adding that "if it's more than that, we'll fight them on it," and adding that the "management and union leadership are both involved in the effort [to improve labor relations]. We recognize our common need to protect the jobs of all employees" (*Arlington Daily News*, February 25, 1986). Shortly thereafter, local plant management stopped production midshift to announce the possibility that the plant could pick up a couple of additional models for production, but that it depended on productivity, quality, and reduced absenteeism (*Arlington Daily News*, March 2, 1986).

By the middle of May 1986, with GM offering to add a new car to the product mix being assembled in Arlington in exchange for more flexible work rules, the members of Local 276 voted overwhelmingly in favor of authorizing their union leadership to reopen negotiations with local management, even though their local labor agreement did not expire until late 1987 (*Arlington Daily News*, May 15, 1986). After almost six months of negotiations, a new labor contract that facilitated adoption of the "Team Concept" was ratified with 87 percent support of voting union members (*Arlington Daily News*, November 14, 1986). The factory's 120 job classifications were reduced to 10, and the seniority system adjusted to form workers into teams of six to twelve who could be cross-trained on all the jobs the team performed, although, as in Janesville, that never occurred. The shop chair called it "a totally different approach" under which "the workers will have more responsibilities, but it should enhance efficiency and quality at the plant" (*Arlington Daily News*, November 11, 1986).

In the wake of the agreement, GM announced that Arlington would not be among the nine plants it was looking to close in 1987, and would instead get new products to assemble, including the Chevy Caprice, Oldsmobile 88, and Cadillac Fleetwood Brougham. In making the announcement, GM's communications coordinator stated that "the plant has raised quality and lowered costs to remain competitive in today's marketplace." The chairman of the bargaining committee for Local 276 shared the sentiment, telling the *Arlington Daily News* that the plant "builds a high quality car, has a good workforce, is successful at holding costs down and has a good management-labor relationship" (*Arlington Daily News*, November 9, 1986), a sharp contrast to the days when Local 276 led all UAW local unions in number of grievances filed.

Arlington versus Ypsilanti: A Public Whipsawing

Five years after their first round of concession bargaining, as GM's declining market share left the automaker with further production overcapacity, the Arlington assembly plant again became vulnerable. At a press conference held a week before Christmas in 1991, GM's chairman announced that the automaker would cut fifteen thousand jobs the following year to reduce its workforce to 289,000 by the end of 1992. In addition, over the following four years GM would close twenty-one factories, including six final assembly plants (*Arlington Daily News*, December 19, 1991), and shed seventy-four thousand jobs (*Arlington Daily News*, February 9, 1992). Finally, instigating perhaps the most blatant, and certainly the most infamous, case of whipsawing autoworkers experienced, the plant in Arlington was specifically pitted against the factory in Ypsilanti, Michigan, even as GM denied any attempt to whipsaw the localities against one another (*Janesville Gazette*, December 20, 1991). Both factories were producing full-sized passenger cars. Assembly would be consolidated into one of the plants. The other would close. GM would announce the fates of the two factories in a few months. Company officials at each location were asked to submit proposals for building 350,000 cars a year (*Arlington Daily News*, December 15, 1991). The competition was on.

GM's announcement sparked a frenzy of activity in Arlington. It was, as an *Arlington Daily News* headline declared, "all or nothing." Survival meant adding 1,200 workers. Closure would cost 3,800 jobs (*Arlington Daily News*, December 15, 1991). Within hours of the announcement, the membership of Local 276 voted, with 82 percent support, to once again reopen contract negotiations with plant management (*Arlington Daily News*, December 22, 1991). GM wanted the authority to add a third shift and operate around the clock, and the union quickly acceded (*Arlington Daily News*, March 1, 1992). The Arlington City Council devised a "victory plan" to keep the plant open (*Arlington Daily News*, December 22, 1991), which included asking the Texas Commerce Department to form an enterprise zone around the plant that would entitle GM to a host of tax exemptions and other economic benefits (*Arlington Daily News*, January 9, 1992). Governor Ann Richards traveled to Arlington to announce that her administration would approve the enterprise zone, and to introduce her own initiative to provide GM incentives to develop alternative fuel vehicles that run on compressed natural gas, to be built in Arlington—an idea that GM never adopted (*Arlington Daily News*, January 12, 1992; February 9, 1992).

At least since the mid-1980s, GM had been subtly forcing local unions to compete for work as it consolidated operations. But the whipsawing of Arlington against Ypsilanti was a watershed moment. As Christopher R. Martin (2004) makes clear in his criticism of the media's reporting at the time, in spite of GM's claims to the contrary, the automaker clearly had "the appropriate information about its own plants to make a decision when it first announced shutdown plans" (80). But by whipsawing the plants, GM gained concessions from the local union, community, and state it would not have otherwise received. In addition, by selecting the Texas plant rather than the Michigan facility that was closer to suppliers and had more modern equipment, which industry analysts at the time predicted would save it (*Janesville Gazette*, February 24, 1992), the company sent a clear message to all workers, unions, and local and state governments that concessions matter. As one worker in Arlington recalled, "They [the workers in Ypsilanti] were shocked and we were shocked. Nobody thought we would stay open." But while she described their approach in Arlington as "what can we do to save ourselves?" the local union and community in Ypsilanti had mostly determined that, in the words of Michigan's Governor John Engler, "what we are not going to do is get into an incentives war to pay them [GM] to work here" (*New York Times*, January 12, 1992).

The explicit and public manner in which GM whipsawed the workers in Ypsilanti against those in Arlington, and perhaps the fact that the automaker selected the plant in Texas over the Michigan facility in "the UAW's own backyard," as one worker in Arlington put it, set off a short firestorm of protest. One national UAW vice president warned that GM was "playing with fire" by pitting the plants against one another and explicitly stated that Local 276 had succumbed to whipsawing for agreeing to twenty-four-hour production (*Arlington Daily News*, March 1, 1992). Round-the-clock production never actually materialized at Arlington, as the popularity of full-sized passenger vehicles continued to decline.

In 1996, GM halted production of large passenger cars in Arlington and converted the plant to assemble their expanding lineup of popular full-sized SUVs. Once the factory was upgraded as part of the redesign of the SUV platform in 2000, Arlington became a popular destination for workers transferring from closing factories, just as Janesville had a few years earlier. By 2004, management claimed that half the workforce had transferred to Arlington in the preceding four years, with a human resource manager suggesting that "there are eighty-two different [UAW] locals represented in this plant."

The very public whipsawing of Arlington against Ypsilanti had cemented for Local 276 a negative reputation throughout the UAW. Workers in Janesville, many oblivious to the reality that their own Local 95 was one of the first unions in the country to succumb to whipsawing, routinely blamed the local union in Arlington for "giving away the store." One woman with nearly thirty years' seniority in Arlington reflected that, within the UAW, "we're the red-headed stepchild down here trying to save our jobs." She knew the perspective of the transferees from other states that Local 276, in the words of one Michigan native who relocated there, "just keeps giving and giving and giving, so they can have jobs, jobs, jobs. And there's no end. Whatever General Motors wants, because they'll sell their mother to keep the jobs in Arlington—with total disregard for the workforce." In response, that Arlington native said "the first question we ask them is, 'Is your plant still open?' And that shuts them up." At the same time, she felt that "the union needs to stop looking at it [the local collective bargaining agreement] as a book of suggestions" and regretted that "we've forgotten about the fight between the union and GM. Now we fight each other." And GM knew that "if you can get the kids fighting amongst themselves, they won't be fighting you."

Diverging Trajectories in Arlington and Janesville

Since the 1980s, as the globalization of the North American auto industry brought new competition to the U.S. automobile market and the spread of lean production, both of the local unions representing workers in the Janesville and Arlington plants succumbed to whipsawing. For both plants, it began in 1986. In Janesville, uncertainty over the future of the plant caused 1,200 workers to relocate to Fort Wayne, Indiana. In the wake of their move, and with an equal number of new hires, local management and the leadership of Local 95 rewrote their contract to embrace the Jointness program and the teamwork, participation, and labor-management cooperation seen as key to future competitiveness. In Arlington, GM first gained concessions by insinuating that the factory would be left without a product to build a few years down the line. Then, by explicitly pitting Arlington against Ypsilanti, GM gained further concessions from Local 276, as well as the local and state governments.

As a result of the whipsawing, GM regained control over the shop floor by scaling back work rules and workplace rights that might otherwise prevent them from implementing lean production. Perhaps more important, GM coerced local unions into adopting productivity as their own goal and the language of cooperative labor relations as their own discourse. All the while, labor contracts maintained GM's traditional right to organize production as it saw fit. Workers were invited to participate, but GM maintained control. This would become vital to the company as it gained the technological capacity to choreograph routines that kept workers in near constant motion.

Still, as Chapter 2 demonstrated, the factories in Janesville and Arlington did not implement the GMS identically. In Arlington, teamwork and employee participation took hold, while in Janesville implementation was superficial. These differences can be attributed to each plant's unique history and their diverging future prospects. In particular, the sudden abandonment of the Jointness program in Janesville in the early 1990s made the automaker's later calls for teamwork and participation under the GMS appear hollow. Furthermore, by 2005 the Janesville facility was widely regarded as too old for GM to invest in retooling for production beyond 2012. In Arlington, however, hope for long-term production remained as long as the plant met GM's goals and stayed in the automaker's good graces at corporate headquarters. This provided incentive for local management, the local union, and its members to implement the GMS in a way their counterparts in Janesville were unwilling or unable to do.

Upheaval and the End of Jointness in Janesville

By all accounts, the cooperative labor relations that had been carefully cultivated in Janesville over the latter half of the 1980s, and which were widely credited with convincing GM to save the plant and award it the new Chevy Suburban assembly line, were destroyed by the automaker in a massive managerial overhaul at the plant during the startup of that new assembly line. The initial startup of a new assembly line, referred to as "the build," involves working out all the kinks to reach full production. The build of the Chevy Suburban assembly line started in April 1991 with 500 workers assembling pilot vehicles. Commercial production was scheduled to begin that August, and gradually increase to forty-four trucks an hour by March 1992 (*Janesville Gazette*, April 16, 1991). That goal, however, was repeatedly pushed back, as plant management stuck to a philosophy of building in-station and working through all the quality issues, even if doing so delayed full productivity. The plant manager was dedicated to implementing the Jointness program, explaining that "it's harder to stick to that concept when you're in the throes of just getting running, then have to stop for quality reasons. But if we set that pattern now, it will be a heck of a lot easier to hold later" (*Janesville Gazette*, January 25, 1992).

General Motors determined it could not wait. Triggered by a 13.5 percent decline in sales that brought the automaker's U.S. market share down to 35 percent (*Janesville Gazette*, December 12, 1991), GM lost $4.5 billion in 1991, a record annual loss for a U.S. business at the time (*Janesville Gazette*, February 24, 1992). In response, GM announced the restructuring plan that included whipsawing the Arlington and Ypsilanti plants against one another. Though the Janesville plant was insulated from the risk of closure due to recent renovations to build the Suburban, it was subject to thinning of the managerial ranks as GM's chairman strived to "lean up the organization" (*Janesville Gazette*, February 10, 1992). With the build of the Suburban assembly line behind schedule, that local shakeup began at the top.

In May 1992, the plant manager in Janesville was replaced (*Janesville Gazette*, May 7, 1992) as part of a purge of senior management that scuttled the cooperative labor relations that local management had cultivated with the union leadership. The new plant manager arrived with a mandate to focus on productivity. One Janesville supervisor who survived the managerial overhaul recalled the chaos that ensued: "They took our plant manager and basically walked him out the front door and said 'stay off the property.' He was the plant manager for five years—Gone. Assistant plant manager and general superintendents—Gone. Superintendents—Gone. Personnel director—Gone. They brought in a guy [to be plant manager] from Linden [NJ], and a new production manager from Rockport, New York, who was here for one reason—get the product out the goddamn door. And that was the game." The impact on labor relations and the Jointness program was immediate: "Working together. Jointness. They could give a rat's ass. If Jointness got in the way of the bottom line, get out of the way. As far as joint meetings at the plant level, floor, formally—nonexistent. Quality councils, joint leadership committee—not meeting. Talk to me in negotiation time. We've got to build product." In fact, full production was not achieved until December 1992, ten months later than originally planned (*Janesville Gazette*, January 30, 1993).

The scuttling of Jointness by Janesville's new plant manager provoked a backlash against the local union leaders who had encouraged the workers to embrace cooperative labor relations. As that supervisor recalled, "Oh Christ, it was ugly. We had a [union shop] chairman that basically went nuts trying to save this place in the mid-eighties," and the behavior of the new plant management "promoted the old way, the old guard" within the union. Those who had criticized Local 95's leadership for their efforts to cooperate in Jointness even as GM demanded concessions and whipsawed plants against one another claimed vindication. They said, "'See, we told you this joint stuff wasn't going to work.' So we took ten steps back. We went back to the traditional adversarial, shop committee, shop chairman 'you want to fight, let's fight, god darnit'" system of labor relations.

GM's abandonment of Jointness ended any hope that lean production might enhance the quality of work in the plant. By the end of 1993, the same shop chair who had urged cooperation with General Motors in the late 1980s again negotiated with the local management radical changes to their collective bargaining agreement. The "modern operating agreement" included a provision that would allow GM to implement the predecessor to the GMS, which the company was calling the "Team Concept."

In theory, workers would be organized into teams, cross-trained on each other's jobs, and determine how best to perform their jobs. Yet, unlike previous calls to embrace Jointness, the shop chair urged the membership to ratify the agreement as necessary to secure their jobs, telling the local press "there's only so much to build, and there are too many plants. If we can't give them a plan to build their trucks and Pontiac can or Flint can or Fort Wayne can, they'll get the work, and we'll get the crumbs" (*Janesville Gazette*, December 19, 1993). Still, the membership initially rejected his plea, defeating the new contract by about 4 percent of the 3,100 votes cast (*Janesville Gazette*, December 22, 1993). Several weeks later, workers overwhelmingly ratified a similar agreement instituting the Team Concept, but which maintained a key component of the plant's seniority system entitling workers to examine and reject job transfers (*Janesville Gazette*, February 9, 1994).

In the wake of the experiment in Jointness, the Team Concept never took hold in Janesville. In part, provisions of the labor contract instituting job rotation on a voluntary basis doomed the practice, since coordinating rotating and nonrotating workers along a moving assembly line is nearly impossible. Furthermore, cross-training workers in each other's jobs took a back seat to production demands as the popularity of large SUVs soared beyond the plant's capacity. Moreover, though without a formal announcement, GM abandoned the model of autonomous teams that determined how to perform their jobs that the automaker had experimented with at its Saturn assembly facility (Cornette 1999; Rubinstein and Kochan 2001; Shaiken, Lopez, and Mankita 1997). Under the GMS, workers would have no discretion over how to perform their jobs, just the opportunity to share their ideas. But because the Team Concept never took hold in Janesville, workers often did not distinguish between the Team Concept and the GMS, both of which were often considered little more than jargon. As one line operator commented in 2004, "We have the team concept, but it doesn't mean anything."

Indeed, on the shop floor the abandonment of Jointness brought an end to the cooperative, team-based organization of work that GM would, years later, claim to be nurturing through the GMS. The '86ers often saw this most explicitly because they were hired into the Janesville plant during the Jointness era, which led many in Janesville to speculate that GM manipulated workers to move to Fort Wayne so that they could hire 1,200 inexperienced workers to kick-start Jointness. Some '86ers reminisced about how well they worked with their supervisors at that time, but that much had changed under the GMS, as determining work routines became the purview of industrial engineers. One '86er complained that, back when she was hired,

> if your job was bad, you could complain to your coworkers and band together. And maybe a group of you went to the foreman and told the foreman what you want[ed] to do, and the foreman would say "OK, try it." That doesn't happen anymore. Even if the whole line went up to the foreman, he would look at you like a scared little rabbit and say "Go back to work, do your job."
>
> They're actually managing different. When we hired in, the line foreman had a lot of authority, could make a lot of decisions as far as manpower, job placement, fixing things that he sees as wrong with the process. Now that's not the system. Line foremen are gophers. They're no different than me—they're just management oriented. There are very few line foremen down there that have any real authority. Their whole role is just to report back to someone else.

Her coworker, also an '86er and a former union committeeman, agreed that "floor foreman now don't stick up for the line people like they used to. They don't go to bat for their workers like they used to. And it's a sad thing." Instead, they say "'I can't stick up for you. I'll lose my job.'" As he explained, there was a perceived lack of trust of workers among supervisors who feared for their own jobs: "'Management' in my opinion, doesn't want to trust anyone. . . . Some of the old management was also hoping to listen to the issues, whatever the issue was. The new management, now, their answer is 'I can't do anything. It's out of my hands. It's above me. That's not my call.' The new management now, they don't manage. They're scared for their jobs. A lot of them are."

In the years after the managerial overhaul in Janesville, and the end of the plant's experiment with cooperative labor relations, consumer demand for SUVs became the driving force behind developments at the plant. Rather than cut the number of workers on the Suburban assembly line from 3,300 to 2,800 over two shifts, as the new plant manager had hoped (*Janesville Gazette*, May 7, 1992), the emphasis changed to increasing production. Janesville soon became a destination for 550 transferees from Michigan, Missouri, and New York, among other places, whose plants were closed as part of the downsizing announced in 1991 (*Janesville Gazette*, October 26, 1994). A deal between GM and the UAW allowed 150 Janesville natives to return from Fort Wayne (*Janesville Gazette*, September 7, 1992; October 1,

1992), somewhat bitter for the experience and for having lost their seniority in the Janesville hierarchy.

In spite of the added workers, by 1994 the plant often operated six days
a week with two ten-hour shifts in an effort to catch up to demand, as
consumers waited at least twelve weeks for delivery of a Chevy Suburban.
Exhausted by the mandatory overtime, and in a rare position of leverage as
the only workers assembling the Chevy Suburban, 92 percent of those voting authorized Local 95 to call a strike demanding the plant hire more workers because "people are working too many hours, and it's affecting safety"
(*Janesville Gazette*, November 6, 1994). The strike was averted when GM
agreed to hire 500 new line operators by letting each worker refer one person to the company, and then selecting applicants by lottery (*Wall Street
Journal*, February 21, 1995). An additional 150 workers were added from that
pool in late 1995. A seven day strike in 1996 over staffing levels resulted in
the hire of yet another 350 workers (*Janesville Gazette*, November 7, 1996)
who had submitted applications two years earlier, some of whom had given
up hope that they would be hired. One worker recalled that he had moved
to California more than a year after submitting his application. But when
GM called his parents' house in Janesville, he packed up his car and drove
through the weekend to report to work on Monday because it was still the
best chance he had at earning a middle-class income.

By the late 1990s, approximately forty-eight hundred people worked
on two different assembly lines in the Janesville plant. Roughly twelve
hundred line operators built medium-duty trucks and the other thirty-
six hundred assembled the SUVs. Only one-third of the labor force had
been working in the plant since before the call for Jointness in the mid-
1980s. Another twelve hundred workers were '86ers hired on a temporary
basis, but whose jobs had become permanent. One thousand workers had
been hired since 1995 due to the explosion in demand for SUVs. The
remaining one thousand workers had transferred from other cities to
take the available, often most arduous, jobs on the Janesville assembly
line. The plant had not been able to simultaneously cut employment and
maintain productivity as GM had hoped, but product demand and quality
remained high (*Janesville Gazette*, May 26, 1995).

While the Jointness program had been abandoned, the concessions that
Local 95 had made to their local collective bargaining agreement were a
lasting legacy. Management had the latitude they needed to standardize
routines and intensify the pace of work. As GM's difficulties persisted and

their plant aged, many workers in Janesville considered themselves lucky to have jobs and viewed maintaining productivity as key to keeping their plant open. By 2004, local union leaders had long since adopted a cooperative tone toward management and were promoting productivity and quality. More than one union committeeperson reported spending more time cajoling their members back to work than filing grievances against supervisors as they used to do. One zoneman bragged of being nicknamed "The Boot" due to his penchant for "kicking ass"—not of supervisors, but of the workers he represented. And several workers suggested the only way they really knew of the latest concession to management was when they called their committeeperson to complain and were told, "Oh yeah. They can do that now." Over less than twenty years, GM had reasserted control over production and changed the behavior of the union to focus on productivity and quality in the hope of saving their members' jobs.

The End of the Line in Janesville

In 2002, Janesville's assembly line building medium-duty trucks was moved to Flint, Michigan, leaving the plant operating a single assembly line for the first time since before the Great Depression. Even as local officials talked of replacing it with another product, the real concern was that GM not shut the plant altogether. With the announcement in 2004 that the automaker would invest $175 million in the plant to prepare for assembly of the next generation of SUVs, the factory received a reprieve that might have extended production until 2012, had there been sufficient customer demand to keep Janesville, Silao, and Arlington busy. Yet it was common knowledge that if demand fell, as it did precipitously a few years later, Janesville would be the first of the three plants to close. In addition, the company indicated that the paint department would need to be entirely replaced if the plant were to stay open beyond 2012, a prospect few imagined likely in a plant approaching its one-hundredth birthday.

The threat of plant closure motivated workers and management alike to push productivity, lest they provide GM an incentive to shut the factory. But the lack of a long-term future served as a disincentive to attempt the changes necessary to implement other aspects of the GMS. Workers doubted the sincerity of the automaker's renewed interest in teamwork and participation, a suspicion substantiated by local management's lack of action on these fronts. Unlike in Silao and Arlington, workers in Janesville were not trained in the philosophy and elements of the GMS. Workers were not permitted to use the Andon system as they had been instructed when it was installed. Management did not trust them to do so, and felt greater pressure to maintain production. Moreover, though they talked about the GMS, local plant management never challenged the union leadership to alter the seniority system to facilitate functional teams. Instead the focus was limited to standardizing routines through which productivity and quality kept improving, year after year, as downtime was eliminated.

This lack of motivation to overcome obstacles to full implementation of the GMS was acknowledged by the president of Local 95 when he suggested that they could implement all the aspects of the GMS found in Silao if GM made a long-term commitment to the Janesville workforce. "We can do it," he insisted, "if they build us a new plant." He was probably correct. The workers would have done anything to get GM to commit to long-term production in Janesville, as would the city and the state. However, without any such hope for the future, GM was losing its capacity and interest to motivate such organizational change in a plant that was ultimately closed in late 2008.

An Uncertain, but Potential, Future in Arlington

In spite of the whipsawing experienced in Arlington, implementation of the GMS there was more thorough than in Janesville, in part because the plant still had long-term prospects and this fact shaped the behavior of both management and labor. As at nearly all GM's plants in the United States, the possibility of closure was real, but it did not represent the immediate threat posed by the age of the plant in Janesville. In fact, since beginning assembly of GM's then hot-selling SUVs in the mid-1990s, the Arlington plant had become a popular destination for transferees looking to resettle and maintain employment with GM. But unlike in Janesville, where there was no GMS training, those transferring to Arlington received two weeks training before starting work "to orient them to what we do here at Arlington," according to one manager. They then joined a work team among a group of workers willing to help out, many of whom were also hoping Arlington would be the last place to which they relocated.

This prospect of longevity provided incentives for workers, their union, and management alike to navigate the most palatable way to implement the GMS—given the intensified pace of the assembly line and the broader competitive context. And so in Arlington, teamwork took on a compromised form. In a manner similar to, but perhaps less extensive than the situation Steven Vallas (2006) describes in his research on workplace change in five paper mills, workers shaped the GMS in a manner that allowed them to support one another and perhaps make their work a little easier. Team coordinators provided service to team members and responded to their problems when the Andon cord was pulled. As in Janesville, workers avoided telling management how to improve productivity, which they associated with harder work and decreased employment. But unlike in Janesville, they did not eschew the suggestion program altogether. Instead, encouraged by management and their union, they focused their suggestions on those ideas that would cut costs and contribute to keeping their plant competitive while also earning them bonuses.

Weakened Unions and Declining Working Conditions in the U.S. Auto Industry

For assembly-line workers in Janesville and Arlington, the globalization of the North American auto industry changed the dynamic of local labor relations to ultimately manufacture consent for the standardization and intensification of work along the assembly line. The loss of market share by Detroit automakers to Japanese automakers created both an incentive and an opportunity for them to gain concessions in work rules and workplace rights from local unions desperate to save local jobs. Left with an overcapacity of production, GM used the threat of plant closure to whipsaw local unions against one another in a competition to match the productivity at the nonunion transplants. In short order, the hegemonic factory regimes of the Fordist era, under which labor gained concessions in exchange for its continued production, gave way to hegemonic despotic regimes in which unions made concessions to working conditions and were co-opted into adopting management's goals of improved productivity.

By the time the GMS was being introduced at GM's factories in the United States, the local unions in Janesville and Arlington had years earlier been whipsawed into concessions so that the automaker could experiment with its previous attempts at lean production. Arguably, had the GMS hinged on teamwork and employee participation, and had these elements actually improved working conditions on the assembly lines, the whipsawing that occurred in Janesville, Arlington, and across GM's factories might be seen as a necessary evil to force the cooperative labor relations on which lean production is said to depend. But in light of the fact the GMS actually revolved around standardized work routines that kept line operators moving for up to fifty-five seconds of each minute, it is clear that the acquiescence of local unions to GM's demands for flexibility reflected a shift in labor relations across the auto industry that has strengthened management's hand to labor's detriment. Once-strong local unions have shifted from policing auto plants to enforce work rules negotiated with the automakers to regulating their own members to encourage productivity, quality, and cooperation with management as they perform their high-paced, standardized routines.

There are, of course, differences between plants. The localities where value chains touch down have unique experiences of globalization. In Arlington and Janesville, GM's strategy of whipsawing plants against one another forced the concession from the local labor unions that the automaker would eventually need to intensify work. However, local conditions resulted in divergent implementation of the rest of the GMS. In Janesville, GM's abandonment of Jointness in the early 1990s, combined with the factory's decreasing viability as it aged, left little will among management and labor to figure out a way to meaningfully implement teamwork and participation. In Arlington, however, even in a plant filled with embittered transferees from around the country, a more complete implementation of the GMS was being negotiated into place.

Overall, autoworkers in the North American auto industry have fewer rights and protections on the shop floor than they did in the Fordist era. In unionized auto plants like those in Janesville and Arlington, where workers have lived this transition, they sacrificed working conditions under pressure to remain competitive. For other line operators, such as those in Silao, who never worked under detailed labor contracts, globalization brought new opportunity rather than whipsawing. There, in Mexico, the GMS and its standardized routines were fully implemented through a very different set of labor relations. It is to the manufacture of consent under that labor regime that I turn next.

4

Greenfield Opportunity

Orchestrated Labor
Relations in Silao

While GM manufactured consent for the standardization and intensification of assembly work in Janesville and Arlington by whipsawing
concessions from the local labor unions and their members, the automaker
cultivated consent for the same work among a young and inexperienced
workforce in Silao. Similar to Asian and European automakers establishing greenfield sites in the United States, in Silao GM took advantage of
the opportunity to establish labor relations and production norms among
an eager young workforce, grateful for the good jobs associated with
auto work.

However, rather than operate nonunion as the transplants did in the
United States, GM worked closely with a Mexican union that embraced
labor-management cooperation so thoroughly that one elected official
calmly explained that "I love my wife. I love my daughter. I love General
Motors. And I love my union. And I see no contradiction in any of that."
Line operators at GM's new plant in Silao would get the best unskilled
blue-collar jobs the area had to offer, but jobs that came with no effective

avenue for dissent. From the outset in Silao, GM maintained tight control over the shop floor and the organization of work. Additionally, GM coordinated labor relations among its local supply chain to suppress wage growth and maintain the automaker's status as the premier local employer.

To convey the thoroughness with which GM manufactured consent in Silao, this chapter begins by recounting the manner in which GM's value chain "touched down" (Bair and Gereffi 2003, 143) in Silao as a development project of Guanajuato state policymakers determined to bring good jobs to the region. The chapter then recounts how GM structured local labor relations to support and reinforce the precepts of lean production by handpicking a union to represent the workers at GM and some of the automaker's local suppliers, one that eschewed labor militancy and espoused a philosophy of labor-management cooperation. Within GM's plant, the union provided services to its members, but ones that complemented GM's own need to maintain low labor turnover and fully implement the GMS. The chapter then places the labor relations in GM's facility within the context of a labor relations regime that GM coordinated among its local supply chain, under which the plants rationalized labor by dividing the local labor market by education and sex and maintained a pay hierarchy among the factories.

The chapter concludes by examining the development paradox in Silao. On the one hand, as state policymakers intended, autoworkers in Silao gained employment with wages and job security unmatched in the region, offering many of them a standard of living unattainable before the arrival of the new plant. On the other hand, Silao might not be experiencing quite the economic development commonly associated with the auto industry. Much like in the United States, the relative good fortune of GM's employees compared to other workers masked a manipulation of organized labor to prevent the labor militancy through which autoworkers have historically gained steadily rising standards of living that have made the auto industry a driver of economic development (Silver 2003).

Luring GM as a Development Project

Workers in Silao owed the arrival of GM and the subsequent growth of a local automotive sector directly to two components of the globalization of the North American auto industry. First, as the Mexican federal government abandoned import substitution industrialization strategies that protected and promoted specific domestic industries to instead adopt neoliberal policies embracing trade and unregulated markets, automakers in Mexico quickly shifted to production for export to the United States (Doh 1998; Holmes 1993; Pries 2000; Ramirez de la O 1998). To meet growing demand, GM, Ford, Chrysler, Volkswagen, and Honda all invested in new assembly plants in Mexico in the 1990s (Humphrey and Memedovic 2003). Second, as a consequence of the widespread adoption of lean production, automakers had become increasingly dependent on key suppliers responsible for coengineering automotive components and delivering them on a just-in-time basis (Helper 1995; Helper, MacDuffie, and Sabel 2000; Veloso 2000). This close relationship between automakers and their first-tier suppliers frequently required auto parts manufacturers to locate factories in close proximity to final assembly plants (Humphrey 2000). With the Mexican federal government focusing on opening markets, economic development policy making shifted to the Mexican states, which vied with one another to attract new final assembly and parts plants.

The state of Guanajuato was among the first to develop policies to take advantage of Mexico's new engagement with the global economy. In 1992, Governor Vicente Fox, a former Coca-Cola executive and future Mexican president (2000–2006), established the Coordinadora de Fomento al Comercio Exterior del Estado de Guanajuato (COFOCE), also known as the Guanajuato World Trade Commission. Operating under the state's secretary of sustainable economic development, COFOCE was charged with promoting exports of products made in Guanajuato and also attracting foreign direct investment to the state. In much the same way that states in the United States attracted new auto plants, COFECE encouraged companies to build factories in Guanajuato by offering them combinations of cash, tax abatements, land, assistance with training, and infrastructure upgrades, depending on the number of jobs that would be created, the level of the investment, the location, and the technology to be utilized.

In interviews, officials at COFECE explained that they devised a plan to industrialize based on their understanding of "follow sourcing" (Humphrey and Memedovic 2003) within the automotive value chain. Policymakers reasoned that if they could convince an automaker to build an assembly plant in Guanajuato, auto parts suppliers would follow, especially if provided incentives to do so. This process began to take shape in earnest in the early 1990s, when GM announced it was investigating possible locations for a new assembly plant. Finding themselves in competition with several other states vying for the jobs GM's new plant would create, and especially with Durango, which COFECE officials believed to have been the preferred location of Mexico's then president Carlos Salinas de Gortari (1988–94), Guanajuato state policymakers began wooing the automaker. First, they produced for GM a labor market feasibility study to convince the automaker of the availability of a young and inexpensive workforce in and around Silao. State officials then offered the automaker a host of incentives to seal the deal. The state purchased the land on which the plant was to be built, gave it to GM, and subsidized the property taxes. They aided GM in obtaining construction licenses to build the facility. The state also upgraded local infrastructure, including construction of highways and Silao's airport.

Once General Motors committed to the site, policymakers began the second phase of their development strategy by targeting GM's suppliers. As anticipated, this process was simplified by the automaker's own expectation that several of its suppliers would locate factories nearby. GM explicitly requested that state officials find an area "in their backyard" for suppliers to build factories. In response, state officials encouraged a local architect to alter his plans to build housing for GM's new employees in Silao, and instead construct the Fipasi Industrial Park.

Filling the industrial park began with a meeting that GM hosted for its suppliers and state officials. The auto parts manufacturers then negotiated with the state for incentives to locate in Silao, including subsidies for the purchase of land and tax breaks. A few businesses were promised cash payments for each job created. One firm, American Gear & Axle, received ongoing subsidies to train its new employees for three months at the State of Guanajuato Institute of Training for Work. In addition, the state improved roads between the industrial park and the GM plant.

Through these efforts, state policymakers convinced a number of GM's suppliers to locate in and around Silao. Several were former subsidiaries of GM that had been spun-off as the automaker adopted lean production and deverticalized its supply chains to focus on automotive design, marketing, and final assembly (Veloso 2000). American Gear & Axle, which had once been a division of GM, built a factory to forge and assemble axles for GM in Silao and for one of the automaker's truck plants in the United States. Delphi, which GM had spun off at the end of the 1990s, and which subsequently became one of Mexico's largest private sector employers (Soden

Table 4.1
Products and key employment statistics of firms in GM's Silao supply chain

Company	Product/service	Year opened	Number of workers	Average age of workers	Approximate weekly salary (U.S. dollars)	Percent women	Annual labor turnover rate	Educational level of workforce	Training time required	Percent of sales to GM-Silao
General Motors	Assembly of Chevy Suburban and Avalanche, Cadillac Escalade	1994	3,400	27.5	130	<5	5.00%	9th grade	12 weeks	
American Gear & Axle	Manufacture of axles	2000	640	24	78	18–20	2.90%	High school graduate	3+ months	75
Aventec	Stamping of doors and hoods	2000	400	25.5	65	0	24%	9th grade	2 weeks	80–90
Oxford Automotriz	Cut steel for stamping	1998	70	29	65	0	2.50%	9th grade	2+ weeks	75
Seglo	GM plant parts handler	1994	800	N/A	65	N/A	High	9th grade	N/A	100
Arela (Delphi)	Manufacture of wire harnesses	1996	1,400	20	45	>95	72%	6th grade	2 weeks	100

Autolog (Delphi)	Sequence parts for just-in-time delivery	1996	480	20	45	20	140%	6th grade	1 week	100
Lear	Manufacture of seats (sewing)	1999	547	21	50	85	23.40%	6th grade	1–2 weeks	100
Lear	Manufacture of seats (assembly)	1999	806	21	65	10	9.36%	6th grade	1–2 weeks	100

SOURCES: Compiled from interviews with human resource managers at each of the plants.

et al. 2001), operated two facilities. The first, Autoensambles y Logisticas (Autolog), was a material handling warehouse that sorted parts delivered from outside the region for just-in-time delivery to GM's local plant. The second, Arneses Eléctricos Automotrices (Arela), built two factories, side by side, between the Fipasi Industrial Park and GM's plant. Both Arela factories assembled the bundles of electrical wiring that run through an automobile, known as wire harnesses, exclusively for GM's Silao facility. Oxford Automotriz, a Michigan-based company, opened a plant in the Fipasi Industrial Park to cut coils of steel into uniform blanks to be fed into GM's stamping machinery. Lear, also based in Michigan, situated a factory twenty miles down the highway between Silao and León that manufactured all the seats needed at GM's plant in Silao. Finally, a Mexican-Japanese joint venture called Aventec opened a plant that stamped and assembled doors and hoods for both GM and Nissan. In addition, GM contracted out material handling within its assembly plant to a German company called Seglo. Table 4.1 details the different products and services included in GM's local supply chain in Silao in 2003, and compares key employment statistics between the plants.

As anticipated by state policymakers, a couple of second-tier suppliers located in the Fipasi Industrial Park as well. According to one executive at United States Manufacturing de México, they were "invited" by American Gear & Axle to open a factory in Silao to produce parts for the truck axles being shipped to the United States. Lagermex built a facility across the street from Aventec, to which it delivered steel blanks for Aventec's stamping presses. In addition, as the state's development strategists had hoped, several factories that were not part of GM's supply chain were successfully enticed to the Fipasi Industrial Park. Grupo Antolín built a factory to produce interior door and roof panels in a building next to Autolog. Continental Teves began production of sensors for antilock braking systems in a new factory across the street from American Gear & Axle. Including a Case factory producing tractors and a Weyerhauser plant making cardboard boxes, the Fipasi Industrial Park hosted ten manufacturing facilities, eight in the auto parts industry, with room for more.

By 2003, Silao's local automotive sector employed approximately nine thousand production workers, seven thousand of whom worked for firms in GM's value chain. Workers earned between $45 and $130 U.S. a week, depending on the company for which they worked, the product they made, and their educational qualifications. In addition, thousands of jobs had been created in factories with no relationship to GM that opened in the wake of the automaker's arrival, as well as through the construction of roads, hotels, the airport, and other businesses prospering from the expansion of manufacturing. Additional construction of new factories was ongoing in the Silao vicinity.

The "New Labor Culture" in Silao

GM's new plant in Silao replaced an older facility in Mexico City that had been experiencing a decade of labor unrest, which made it part of a trend in the country. As automakers shifted to production for export, they moved north, and typically well north of Silao, both to be closer to the United States and to establish fresh labor relations (Micheli 1994). Interviews with human resource managers at GM and each of their local suppliers, as well as union officials and workers, revealed how GM crafted labor relations in Silao. As had become customary among new employers in Mexico (Caulfield 2004), upon arriving in Silao, each firm selected, or "recognized," a union to represent the workers they were yet to hire. According to human resource managers, this common practice allowed firms to avoid the "radical" unions that might encourage workers to strike or cause other "problems."

All the firms in GM's local supply chain selected unions affiliated with the Confederation of Mexican Workers (CTM), Mexico's largest trade union confederation. The two smallest plants, Oxford Automotriz and Autolog, each recognized what are known in Mexico as *sindicatos fantasmas* or "ghost unions." Ghost unions do not actually represent workers in any meaningful way, and often exist unbeknown to the workers themselves. Instead, for a fee, ghost unions protect employers by signing labor contracts that offer workers no new wages or benefits, but which legally preclude the workers from organizing their own unions (Greer, Stevens, and Stephens 2007; Plankey-Videla 2012).

GM, American Gear & Axle, Aventec, and Arela, which together employed more than 90 percent of the workers in GM's Silao supply chain, recognized the Sindicato de Trabajadores de la Industria Metal, Mecánica Automotriz, Similares y Conexos (Union of Metal and Automotive Mechanical Workers, or SITIMM by their Spanish acronym), a regional confederation of forty-four workplace-based unions, or "sections," that ranged in size from ten to 3,300 members. According to one SITIMM official, before hiring a single worker, "GM researched the unions that were here in Guanajuato, the history of the union and the type of union they were. They had various interviews with different union representatives. This I conclude because in Mexico City I spoke to the leader of another union, who commented to me that they also had been offered the contract at GM before SITIMM. I asked him what happened and he said, 'I don't know exactly. In the end the company said, 'We're not going with you. We have another union.'" By making the union attractive to employers, SITIMM's leaders had grown the union's membership to slightly over sixteen thousand members since its founding in the early 1980s (Babson 2002).

SITIMM's leaders pitched the union as embodying Mexico's "new labor culture," a slogan emblazoned on its T-shirts and hats. Typical of the unions that automakers were selecting for their plants in Mexico (Bayón and Bensusán 1998; Bensusán 2000), SITIMM was emphatically nonmilitant, with a philosophy that held cooperation and consultation with management to be key to gaining good pay and benefits for workers. According to their annual publication, SITIMM was committed to promoting the interests of its members and raising their standard of living, but with "a philosophy that bears in mind: the current and future circumstances in which we practice unionism; the firms, the products and the markets confronting the firms we serve; the improved opportunities offered by permanent dialogue and communication between the firm, union and workers; the protection of wage increases based on technical argument more than displays of force" (SITTIMFORMA 2001, 3, my translation). According to one human resource manager, this philosophy made SITIMM a union "we can work with." Another praised SITIMM's leadership as "visionary."

At most factories where SITIMM was asked to form a union, the plant's section was run by a committee of workers elected every three years. One of SITIMM's two regional deputy general secretaries described this decentralization of control over policy and resources as unique among unions. He explained that "each worker pays 2 percent of their salary" to the union. "But of the 2 percent, 25 percent is administered in this central office and 75 percent is administered by the committee at their plant." This distribution of funds, he said, reflected "an enormous difference" between SITIMM and other unions within Mexico and the CTM, especially the ghost unions. The fact, he said, that there is a committee in each plant, for us, is fundamental because they are the representatives of their own workers and they have their resources, their money. [It] is very important. So they can do their own work. I believe that inside the CTM we are the union that most leaves their committees to manage their own resources. Others give 50 percent to the central committee and 50 percent to the plants; others 75 percent to the central committee, 25 percent to the plant; and others all to the central committee and very little to the delegates that they have in the plant.

While in theory this decentralized structure delegated to the different sections broad authority, the role that the SITIMM's central office played in establishing and overseeing those sections mitigated actions counter to the labor-management cooperation professed by headquarters.

The manner in which bargaining committees were trained to temper wage demands is illustrative. One SITIMM official involved in negotiations indicated that section leaders often believed their employers could and should pay much higher wages, which he maintained was a misconception based on a lack of experience. Accordingly, it was his job to train inexperienced union negotiators to moderate their demands, a process he described like this: "'Why don't we have more money?' That's what they say because they don't have information. The worker demands 100 percent. That's what they say they deserve—that they need to increase salaries 100 percent. . . . It's impossible. We will shut the plant and everyone will lose their jobs. So, we give them training. We give them courses in collective bargaining. How do we evaluate a decision? You want to raise salaries 100 percent. Let's look at how much money that is." But sometimes the section leaders insisted on taking such demands to their employers and had to learn through negotiations to lower their expectations: "The workers begin to come around themselves, apart from the training we give them. Five days—ten days—there are not negotiations. Fifteen days and there isn't an accord. There is no accord." Eventually, the workers begin to moderate their demands:

"Fine, 80 percent. OK?"
"Fine, 60 percent. OK?"
"Fine, 50 percent . . ."
Until they understand how to negotiate, and more courses, and more training.

Over time, he said, the section bargaining committees learned to make calculations ahead of time, to work with the numbers the company provided them to formulate "reasonable" goals that could be achieved through a collective bargaining process that included no hint of a threat of any type of industrial action by workers. Eventually, he said, "they understand to calculate the numbers: adding, subtracting, dividing, multiplying to know how much, what is possible, what is our objective, what is obtainable? The company: to look at where we can gain from them. What are their possibilities? What is their situation? How is the market? How is the world market? What is their product? How is it positioned in the market? Everything. Everything. Everything. And we give this knowledge to the bargaining committee. It's difficult. Very difficult."

The idea that workers and their employers shared mutual interests permeated SITIMM's literature and meetings. The socialization of workers began during the hiring process itself, which included an interview with union representatives that served as a first indoctrination into the "new labor culture." In fact, SITIMM's job application obfuscated the difference between being a good worker for the firm and being a good union member by asking, for example: "Would you be ready to support your union brothers (or sisters), [by] working overtime, rotating shifts, working holidays, participating in meetings, assemblies, marches, as is required by you in the union statutes?" As was common practice throughout Mexico, union security clauses at the factories in Silao made union membership a condition of employment. Labor militants, or anyone who failed to subscribe to SITIMM's philosophy of labor-management cooperation, could therefore be prevented from gaining employment by denying them union membership (Caulfield 2004; La Botz 1992).

Furthermore, since GM and other firms recognized unions before they even had employees, new workers entered plants that had collective bargaining agreements already in place, signed by the company and the general secretary of SITIMM. Regional union officials would then identify workers they considered "potential leaders," to groom as union delegates and eventually form a union committee within their plant, under continued guidance from SITIMM's main office. According to union officials, it normally took about two years to develop a fully functioning section committee. But it could take longer, particularly at plants with high labor turnover rates, where the workforces lacked the stability necessary to form a committee. In fact, SITIMM officials expressed doubt that the section at

Arela's wire harness plants would ever have its own committee because of the factories' persistently high turnover.

SITIMM Section Four

Workers at GM's plant were represented by SITIMM Section Four, the structure and leadership of which began to take shape almost immediately after the automaker recognized SITIMM. The first employees GM hired received joint training by the automaker and the union before the plant had actually been built. As the deputy general secretary of SITIMM explained:

> GM hired an initial group of fifteen workers that helped out when they [GM] opened an office while the plant was being built, and in this office the workers helped to carry boxes, arrange files and the rest, and began company training about the production system they wanted to implement. Then ... the group began to grow gradually, and they were going to the plant to visualize what would happen. The company wanted this group to be the most experienced and then they could be the basis of training for the other workers.
>
> This initial group, when they went for their company training, I had the responsibility of going to give them union training. I worked many hours with them, many days, going over the history of the workers' movement, the structure of SITIMM and the CTM, the federal labor law, everything, everything, everything.

One of those first employees was the son of SITIMM's general secretary, the highest-ranking union official, and also the brother of the deputy general secretary who did all that training. Clearly overeducated for work on GM's assembly line, he was hired for the express purpose of establishing the union committee that would represent the workers at GM. As he recalled: "I graduated, finished my studies in '91 ... and I began working here in the [union's] office. Then the [union's Executive] Committee determined that as there was a new section [at GM], we had to work hard as a union. I began with the first group of unionized workers [at GM] ... in March of 1992, when the construction of the building and the installation of the equipment and heavy machinery began. And I finished working in January 1996." In coordination with GM, those original workers were spread around the plant to educate workers about the union, its philosophy, and functions:

> The first group arrived in '92. There were eleven of us, and there were only eleven of us for the first eight months. Afterward, they arrived in groups, like fifty, fifty, fifty, and so on. Then, they assigned each of us eleven to an area. Some were sent to assembly, others to the body shop, and in my case, paint. We were on the payroll as workers. I worked for GM. OK? Our work was that when the groups entered we were the union delegates and before they were hired we gave them an induction talk about the union, etc., etc., and we interviewed them. At that time, there were a lot of interviews.

Eventually, the governing committee of Section Four at GM was established with the son of SITIMM's general secretary as its leader. In his words, "In '94 we had a meeting. There was an assembly of all the workers and I was elected to the committee, the first committee at GM." He served as the first general secretary of SITIMM Section Four until deciding not to run for reelection in 1996, a race one GM worker insisted he would have lost, saying, "We may be naïve, but we're not stupid." He then left his job with GM and went back to work at SITIMM's regional headquarters.

The Section Four that first general secretary established and left behind was designed to provide workers services to help them acclimate and take advantage of their newfound steady incomes. It did not represent them in disputes with management or interfere with GM's organization and pace of work. Section Four's governing body was a sixteen-member committee of "secretaries" under the leadership of a general secretary. Each of the union secretaries was responsible for some area of the union's interests, which were defined broadly and often reached beyond the plant. So while the secretary of transportation was in charge of ensuring the buses that delivered the workers to the plant and brought them home after their shift were safe, clean, and prompt, the secretary of agriculture was responsible for agricultural issues. Agriculture, it was explained, was a union issue because it directly affected the local economy and many union members had family who farmed. Of the sixteen secretaries, five worked full-time in the union's office, located immediately off the shop floor and directly next to the plant's human resources office. The other eleven members of the committee carried out their union duties in addition to working on the assembly line, with time allotted to attend meetings or other union business. Like their counterparts at the local unions in Janesville and Arlington, the entire committee remained on GM's payroll.

Union elections were held every three years, with workers voting for slates of candidates led by the worker who would become general secretary. The union has been credited with maintaining "vigorous internal democracy" (Babson 2002, 32). The election I observed was overseen by SITIMM's regional leadership and was painstakingly transparent. Workers voted in the parking lot where the buses dropped them off to start their shift and picked them up at the end of their day. Representatives of each slate of candidates staffed tables lining the edges of the parking lot. Together, they constructed and sealed each ballot box to ensure it was empty before balloting began. During the vote, each worker's identification badge number was cross-referenced with the master list of union members to make sure that all those voting were eligible to do so, that they did so at the correct table, and that workers only voted once. At the end of the day, the ballot boxes were walked to a table at the corner of the parking lot. One by one, and with the candidates for office observing, each box was unsealed, the ballots tallied, and the final results announced.

Upon gaining office, the committee's primary function was to negotiate a new collective bargaining agreement with the automaker every two years, as well as wages and benefits on an annual basis, as prescribed by Mexican labor law. Through these negotiations wages had increased steadily, with a large bump in pay included in the labor agreement negotiated in 2000 (Babson 2002). But these rising wages are better attributed to the automaker's own strategy for reducing labor turnover than to the union's bargaining power or acumen. Even some of the union's enthusiastic supporters acknowledged that SITIMM had little actual bargaining power over the automaker. One simply pointed out that "GM is GM."

However, high rates of labor turnover have been a problem in Mexican auto plants, including GM's plant in Ramos Arizpe (Micheli 1994) and Ford's plant in Hermosillo, both of which were located hundreds of miles closer to the U.S. border than was the plant in Silao. In Hermosillo, where even as the Ford plant won praise for matching the productivity levels and quality of its sister plant in the United States, persistent turnover problems "seriously undermined plans for increasing worker participation, individual training, and multi-skilling" (Carrillo and Montiel 1998, 312). By all accounts, GM's plant in Silao experienced high turnover from the outset as well, and did not begin to stabilize its workforce until higher wage rates were negotiated with the union. According to the SITIMM official who served as the first general secretary of Section Four:

> GM had a lot of turnover. In 1992, when the first collective bargaining contract was issued, it was a contract with the minimum required by law. They paid little, fifteen pesos daily. Many entered, and when they saw the pay: "Bye Bye!" to look for a better job. Now, this was so. And it isn't that the union was saying: "Yes, yes, it has to be so." No. You know that in Mexico today we have a lot of unemployment. So when a firm comes, in practice they establish the minimum conditions, and because we need the work, we have to go to work. Of course, our labor law says that each year we negotiate. So then, after ten years there have been ten negotiations that have led to the salaries and benefits they have now. So, over time, the turnover has diminished. But at the beginning there was a lot.

GM's personnel relations manager in Silao agreed, indicating that by 2002 they had managed to get turnover down to 6 percent from between 9.5 and 10 percent the previous three years.

As described by various members of Section Four's governing committee, the remainder of their duties involved supporting employees as they adjusted to work in a factory and helping them manage their newfound income. Some new employees needed help opening bank accounts and managing a weekly income stream. Many required support and coaxing to take advantage of the federal program through which workers with stable incomes could obtain low-interest mortgages. SITIMM promoted the home ownership program widely, and Section Four not only assisted their members in filling out the paperwork but also maintained the workers' files and made sure they did not miss payments. Union officials explained that home ownership was both a benefit of employment at GM and an incentive to stay employed, lest one lose the income necessary to make mortgage payments.

At times, Section Four's work extended well beyond assistance with financial issues. The union's secretaries also described helping workers and their families deal with crises or just adjust to the changes to family life that accompanied their employment. They visited workers' sick relatives in the hospital, organized funerals for family members of GM's employees, and even claimed to have conducted ad-hoc marriage counseling, for which they acknowledged having no training.

One member of the committee gave an example in which the union was called by a workers' wife: "A spouse of a worker called us because she was concerned that her husband left for work at 11:00 and still had not returned. 'Well, what happened? Where is my husband?' So, we looked into what had happened to him, to see whether he left here at 11:00 in the evening. And they told us that . . . he had stayed to work overtime. So, we called her to let her know that there was no problem; that he would arrive soon." But he also suggested that this situation could have turned out quite differently, requiring the union officials to investigate further. If the worker had left the plant as scheduled and was missing: "He could have been robbed, or who knows. And clearly, even if he had left early, and she was concerned, we would more or less check into what happened. If we find out that he was assaulted, that he was robbed, that he was kidnapped, we have to do something. . . . We have to be concerned because, in the final analysis, it is the well-being of his family. It is his well-being, and if he is not well, then he'll work poorly."

This particular union secretary had been among an early group of workers sent from Silao to train on an assembly line in the United States. (He returned somewhat disillusioned for the reception he received, wondering "what do they have against us?"). Reflecting on the much sharper distinctions between work issues and personal issues drawn by unions in the United States than by SITIMM, he attributed these to their respective economic situations: "In the United States, you have it good. That's the way I see it in every respect. There you have money. There nothing concerns you." In Mexico "because of the economic situation, you have to search for new alternatives to be well or survive."

In interviews, Section Four officials repeatedly returned to this theme, linking union services to workers' job performance and, ultimately, their well-being. In the services they provided, the union hoped to relieve workers of distractions in their personal lives that might otherwise cause their performance to suffer, thereby threatening their employment and livelihood. Through this approach, the union assisted GM in retaining workers and maintaining stable work teams. In fact, in the absence of the union, some of its responsibilities might have fallen on the plant's human resource department. Instead, the union had a niche through which it could serve the needs of both the workers and the automaker. But its impact on wages, benefits, and working conditions appeared minimal.

Recruitment and Training at GM

Working with a union whose philosophy and services complemented GM's own human resource needs, the automaker meticulously screened and trained the workers who would be hired to fill some of the best blue-collar jobs in the region. As the premier employer in the area, GM found itself with no shortage of applicants. The personnel relations manager expressed quite frankly that "GM is GM. That is, it's very attractive to the people in the area." Several line operators indicated that it was not uncommon for them to be stopped in the street by complete strangers, who, upon spotting the GM logo on their shirts, began inquiring how they, too, might gain employment at the plant. The challenge for GM was to select and train those workers who would be most likely to integrate into work teams for the long term and to avoid the problems that Ford experienced opening a greenfield site in Hermosillo. Ford originally targeted applicants with more than a high school education, but persistently high turnover caused the automaker to shift tactics and recruit younger, less educated workers who had lower expectations for continued training and advancement (Carrillo 1995; Carrillo and Montiel 1998; Shaiken 1994, 1990).

In Silao, GM recruited men with a ninth-grade education, instead of the high school and college graduates originally targeted by Ford. The personnel relations manager indicated that "we have basic requirements. To be able to apply you have to have secondary schooling [completed ninth grade] or have finished a technical course. You must have a military release card and be more than eighteen years old. These are the three basic requirements." Those who met these requirements filled out a job application that probed the details of their financial obligations, including how many dependents they supported, whether they rented or owned their home, and the amount of the monthly payments. Company and union officials indicated that the more a candidate could demonstrate a need for a stable income, the more attractive they were to the automaker. The ideal candidate was a young man with a family to support and financial commitments that would tie him to the plant.

Though the personnel relations manager insisted that GM had no pref-
erence for male employees, women comprised only 5 percent of the workforce, suggesting that they were being systematically deselected, either
directly for their sex or indirectly through the application process. This may
have been a reflection of the prevailing attitude, directly expressed by the
human resource manager at one of GM's local suppliers, that women disrupt the "stability" and "smooth functioning" of teams by taking advantage
of the paid maternity leave mandated by Mexican labor law. This might
also explain why, according to one union official, GM had only recently
begun "experimenting" with women on the assembly line.

Assuming their application was in order, the personnel relations manager indicated that applicants underwent an extensive evaluation process:
"This evaluation is not just ability and skill. We also evaluate what we refer
to as 'competence': leadership, work in a team, safety, responsibility. The
candidates go through a series of exercises and interviews and we rate them.
We categorize them as A, B, C. A are those with the highest scores." This
evaluation included tests of literacy and math skills, a personality test, and
perhaps an IQ test. Applicants were also critiqued for their performance in
a mock work environment, as illustrated by the personal relations manager:
"I'll give you an example. We put them to assembly. We give them wheel
rims. We give them instructions. We give them safety equipment and we
put them to work in a team to assemble rims, and they give us very valuable
information." So the applicants were judged not only on their ability to do
the work but also on the way "they react to particular circumstances, [to]
other workers. This is very important. After that, if they pass this application, this filter, then what follows are basic medical exams."

If they passed the initial screening, applicants were offered conditional
employment in the form of a twelve-week training and assessment period,
during which they could be let go at any time. The first eight weeks were
classroom training to socialize applicants and prepare them to join the
workforce as a line operator. According to the personnel relations manager:
"They spend eight weeks getting to know the systems in what we call the
'Silao Production System.' That involves all the systems that they operate:
the comparison system, the safety system, the quality system, the personnel system. Everything is perfectly defined." The union official who served
as the first general secretary of SITIMM Section Four at GM referred to
this first eight weeks of training as "'coco wash.' Yes, brain washing," before
stipulating that "we all accept the system . . . It is lovely to work in a team."

Though the personnel relations manager indicated that GM did not hire workers with previous manufacturing experience so as to avoid having to rid them of "bad habits," training included comparisons of "traditional" and "transformed" manufacturing processes and "traditional" and "modern" organizations. To prepare for working in the modern Silao Production System, new employees spent the bulk of their eight weeks of classroom training learning and practicing the interpersonal skills they would need to work in teams. The 450-page training text distributed to the workers was divided into thirteen sections, with a unit each on Working in Teams, Communicating with Others, Influencing Others, Resolving Conflicts, Reaching Agreement in Teams, Rescuing Difficult Meetings, Participating in Meetings, Valuing Differences, Making the Difference, Toward Empowerment, Empowerment and the Leader, and two on Supervising Effective Meetings.

Upon completion of the eight-week program, applicants began the final phase of training and evaluation by actually joining a work team. As the personnel relations manager emphasized, theory is important, but "above all, they are workers in a team. Our operating system here is based on workers in teams." So the next test was to determine whether they could be "perfectly integrated into the system. By now, they don't have to learn the basics. They now are ready to develop" into regular line operators and team members. Only after successfully integrating into a work team over a four-week period, under the guidance of a team leader, did the assessment period end and the applicant become a full employee, complete with a pay raise to the basic wage in the collective bargaining agreement. However, until that day, "in these twelve weeks containing the principal training, they can be rejected at any moment." The personnel relations manager indicated that approximately one in four applicants who were offered conditional employment actually completed the training and became full employees twelve weeks later.

Coordinated Labor Relations in Silao

While inside the final assembly plant GM and its hand-selected union manufactured consent for the automaker's lean Global Manufacturing System among a carefully selected group of workers, GM's influence over labor relations extended to its entire local supply chain. With the unions in and around Silao hand selected by the employers, either for their dedication to labor-management cooperation or for their low profile altogether, GM and their suppliers were able to coordinate employment practices.

Human resource managers in Silao met monthly. Among the purposes of these meeting was to exchange lists of employees who had recently quit or been fired. Ostensibly, the lists saved the plants from rehiring "poor quality workers," in the words of one human resource manager. Effectively, this meant there was a blacklist that prevented workers from moving from one factory to another in search of new or better jobs. GM and its parts suppliers also coordinated their collective bargaining. For instance, when in 2002 GM sought to cut costs by redistributing the forty-eight-hour week over five days rather than six, each plant negotiated the same provision to avoid disrupting the just-in-time production schedules practiced under lean production.

The arrangement between the plants, however, extended well beyond these moments of cooperation. GM coordinated a local labor relations regime that applied the principles of lean production to labor relations by rationalizing the use of labor throughout the supply chain to maximize overall efficiency, even if it meant compromising productivity at any specific site (Rothstein 2004). The firms divided up the local labor market by sex and educational status. General Motors, Aventec, and Oxford Automotriz each employed men with a ninth-grade education, though GM sprinkled a few women throughout the plant. Arela and Autolog hired workers with a sixth-grade education. Arela employed nearly exclusively women while Autolog's workforce was 80 percent male. Only American Gear & Axle's employees were required to have completed high school or received technical training.

In addition to this parceling out of the labor market, several human resource managers referred to "an unwritten agreement" through which the firms maintained a pay hierarchy among the plants. Accordingly, GM preserved its place as the status employer in the region, paying line operators an average of $130 a week, 50 percent more than those with comparable educational qualifications at Oxford Automotriz and Aventec. One manager at Aventec complained that because "we have to keep our wages below the guys' [American Gear & Axle] across the street," his factory struggled with high labor turnover, so much so that the original director of human resources at the plant was fired for his inability to reduce the 30 to 40 percent monthly labor turnover that nearly crippled production.

Otherwise, the pay scale roughly reflected the educational qualifications of the workers. Autolog and Arela paid their employees around $45 a week. Only at American Gear & Axle, where the average wage was $78 a week,[1] could workers' pay eventually exceed that received by line operators on GM's assembly line, but only after amassing two years' seniority and training for a supervisory position paying up to $200 a week.[2]

This wage hierarchy permeated GM's plant, where the automaker had subcontracted material handling to a German-based logistics firm called Seglo. In Silao, all the off-line jobs delivering parts to the assembly line, so sought after by workers with high seniority in Janesville and Arlington, were performed by workers who were not employed directly by GM. Like GM's workers in Silao, Seglo's eight hundred employees were required to have a ninth-grade education. Yet they earned half as much as the GM line operators receiving those parts. Seglo could absorb the increased labor turnover that accompanied lower pay, because the company's workers were not included in GM's teams and required less training.

Though officials at SITIMM claimed to have complained to GM that the pay hierarchy among the automaker and its suppliers interfered with the union's collective bargaining rights, they indicated that they were powerless to stop the practice. One official suggested it was a common practice, "not only here in Silao. That's the way it is in all of Mexico: PEMEX [the Mexican oil company], petrochemicals, sugar. All the industries are the same."

Still, officials at SITIMM lent tacit credibility to the coordinated labor relations by repeating management's justifications for human resource practices at each plant. This was most blatant at the Arela wire harness plants, where low wages resulted in high turnover that compromised productivity. Arela's human resource manager recruited workers by driving around the small villages, or "ranchos," dotting the countryside in a car with a megaphone on the roof advertising to young women the availability of jobs paying twice the minimum wage. Wiggling their fingers in the air, the human resource manager and SITIMM officials alike, all of whom were men, repeated commonly made assertions that women were uniquely suited to wire harness production due to their "nimble fingers" and "attention to detail" (Plankey-Videla 2012; Salzinger 2003). When I pointed out that Arela's parent company, Delphi, employed men in its wire harness factories in other parts of Mexico, managers at Arela conceded that some men have the dexterity and mind-set conducive to wire harness production. They insisted, however, that local cultural norms prevented them from hiring men in Silao because the female employees would quit, having been forbidden to work alongside men by their husbands, fathers, brothers, and boyfriends. Yet men and women worked together down the road at Delphi's Autolog plant, as well as on the outskirts of León at the Lear seating plant.

Furthermore, the work at Arela was deemed "unskilled" in order to justify the workers' low pay and the company's recruitment practices. Yet the work at Arela required more training than at either Aventec or Seglo, where male workforces were paid higher wages. New hires at Arela trained for two weeks on mock assembly lines called "carousels," learning to decipher the alphanumeric codes indicating which wires to string through the maze of pegs protruding from the plywood plank passing before them as it moved out of reach to the next woman on the assembly line. If trainees scored at least 80 percent on a final exam, they joined a production carousel with anywhere from fifteen to fifty other women, any one of whom could ruin a harness by making a single mistake.

With a 72 percent annual labor turnover rate, there was a constant rotation of new workers onto the assembly lines at Arela. As a result, productivity was so low, and product defect rates so high, that the factory maintained a week's supply of harnesses in inventory as a buffer guaranteeing their ability to meet GM's just-in-time delivery schedule, a practice associated with mass production that is supposed to be anathema to lean production (Womack, Jones, and Roos 1990). Still, neither GM nor the union pressured Arela's management to raise wages and stabilize their workforce, which would have allowed SITIMM to set up a full union committee at the plant. Instead, union officials repeated management's complaints regarding the unreliability and poor work ethic of the rural women who worked there, even as one union delegate at the plant questioned why she and her coworkers earned so much less than GM's employees since "we make cars, too."

Instead, the inefficiencies at Arela and other plants were sacrifices that served GM's larger purpose. Working closely with a union the automaker had handpicked, and its suppliers, some of which were former subsidiaries, GM conspired to manipulate the local labor market by dividing the labor force by education and gender, screening out labor militants or malcontents, and maintaining a wage hierarchy among the plants with the automaker at the top. This simultaneously preserved GM's status as the premier employer in the region, which was important to its manufacture of consent on the assembly line, while controlling wage growth.

Seeds of Discontent in Silao?

While GM had quite successfully crafted a labor relations regime in Silao that fostered labor peace and a wholesale implementation of the GMS, this is not to say that workers were uniformly happy or unaware of the manipulation at hand. In spite of the training workers at GM received to socialize them into the environment of labor-management cooperation, they were not unaware that their union operated at the behest of GM, or that the wages paid at GM's plants in the United States was far higher than their own. Several who were interviewed reasoned that the company could, therefore, afford to pay higher wages in Silao. One worker suggested that doubling the wages in Silao would be fair, saying that while GM had improved the lives of he and his coworkers, if they "would pay us half what they pay in the United States, that would really change our lives."

Skepticism of the union was exacerbated by the fact that, in its short history, Section Four had already seen a leader forced to resign for misappropriating funds. One worker said quite simply that "they stole from us." While SITIMM's regional officials framed their handling of the incident as evidence that the union would not abide corruption, the incident had tarnished the union's reputation among the young workforce. (Exactly what happened was not openly discussed. Upon questioning, officials at SITIMM declined to offer details except to acknowledge that it had occurred and to emphasize that it had been appropriately dealt with rather than being swept under the rug.)

Without any say over the organization of work, and with limited collective bargaining power, the general secretary of Section Four worried about the extent of his ability to represent the workers who elected him. While this research was under way, he and his committee became the first to win reelection to a new three-year term. But their victory was a narrow one, and largely due to the fact that eight other slates of candidates split the opposition vote. The incumbents received only 641 votes, roughly one-quarter of those cast and less than 20 percent of the total membership of Section Four. In the end, they won by eighty votes over the slate that came in second. Having taken over the union's reins only a year and a half early, he disappointedly reflected: "There is no real appreciation for what a union leader does. This is the point that's occurring to me, because, really, we took over for Rafael [who had been removed for stealing the union funds]. He's the only one to this point who has been found guilty of mismanagement. He is the only one, from whom we saved the boat from sinking. To take over a union with sixty-two pesos in union dues, to make it stable with healthy numbers. We do a lot of social work, and to see that, really, the workers didn't vote for us. . . . We got lucky, very lucky." This, in spite of the fact that, compared to previous union committees, he felt that "we pay more attention to the people. There have been a lot of problems on the line. We attend to those more directly, and also don't stop providing service in the office, because previous committees kept the office closed. I have it open both shifts, so you more directly give attention to the worker. Perhaps that is what, in the end, gave us our victory. Though it was a tight victory."

However, recognizing that people will learn something about the dynamics of the union elections, that many of the slates of candidates that ran against him had not worked to garner support throughout the plant, and that in the future the opposition might be less fragmented, he was thinking about what it would take to win reelection again in another three years:

> It makes us think about what we're going to do differently over the next three years, so that the worker that you help, who doesn't see that you are helping them . . . that you get to where the union helps him and he sees that it is the union. That's what didn't exist in this election. A lot of people we help, including those who ran on another slate, are those about whom we say there isn't a union consciousness. And it is a big problem. If it is the same in three years, it will be difficult. . . . So, the challenge that we have is to educate the people, to sensitize them to what a union is: What is the union? What are the workers' fights? Why did they create unions? What is the union's goal? All of this.

Part of his solution was to bring the union in closer contact with the workers on an everyday basis by negotiating a similar role for union representation on the shop floor as was traditional in the United States and other parts of Mexico, precisely the type of role GM had been scaling back in its U.S. plants through whipsawing: "The idea is area delegates, to have them on each line . . . one for the door line, one for the chassis, and to do that throughout the plant." In arguing the legitimacy of the idea, he pointed out that "GM has plants, here in Mexico, that have delegates. This is the only one that doesn't have them." Whether GM would agree to a union presence on the shop floor, he agreed, might become a contentious bargaining issue. He understood that GM was supportive of the union only so long as it did not interfere with the automaker's right to manage the shop floor.

The Silao Experience in Perspective

GM's assembly plant in Silao was no sweatshop. To the contrary, it was a state-of-the-art, clean, and safe facility. GM's employees were among those workers benefiting from the new opportunities offered by globalization. They enjoyed wages, benefits, and stable employment unmatched in the region. Like the governors of states in the United States that had attracted foreign transplant auto factories (Ruckelshaus and Leberstein 2014), policymakers in Guanajuato had brought to the area among the best blue-collar jobs the economy had to offer.

The automaker, however, was not an equal opportunity employer in Silao. Women were mostly excluded from its workforce and those of its highest-paying suppliers. Anyone whose work experience or personality suggested they might support a more vocal form of unionism than that being promoted in the plant was similarly excluded. If they could find employment in the industry at all, these workers were left to find jobs among GM's suppliers, where pay and benefits were determined by a firm's place in the local wage hierarchy, which did not necessarily correspond to the level of skill and training required to perform jobs at those factories. In fact, the jobs were highly gendered, with those performed by women at Autolog deemed to be lowest skilled in spite of evidence to the contrary.

Moreover, local labor relations had, over the decade the plant had existed, been carefully scripted to manufacture consent for the local version of the GMS. SITIMM had doubled its membership by practicing a unionism attractive to employers rather than to workers. Within the context of the wage hierarchy between the plants, the union had little, if any, leverage in collective bargaining. Instead, officials at SITIMM's regional offices coached the bargaining committees of their various sections to moderate their demands. Certainly, the workers could have done worse. Unlike ghost unions, SITIMM provided real services, especially for the members of Section Four at GM's plant.

To be sure, circumstances change. Greenfield sites do not stay greenfield forever. Workers age, gain experience, and their needs change. The leaders at Section Four were already struggling to better represent their members in order to stay in office. At least in theory, the democratic structure of the union opens the possibility of more militant workers winning election. Yet Mexican labor relations are infrequently transparent, and GM would likely have avenues to diffuse such a movement. In fact, sometime after fieldwork in Silao was completed, the union within GM's assembly plant disaffiliated from SITIMM and instead joined another CTM union that also claims the union at Ford's plant in Hermosillo as an affiliate. Exactly why this occurred is not clear. (When contacted, an official at SITIMM's headquarters indicated there had been a disagreement between the general secretary of Section Four and the leadership of SITIMM.) Given the automaker's influence and the manner in which unions come to be recognized by employers in the region, however, it seems unlikely the move took place without GM's consent, if not at the automaker's behest.

GM's operations in Silao offer a paradox. On the one hand, the automaker offered the best blue-collar jobs in the region, and was largely responsible for thousands of other jobs among local suppliers. On the other hand, the local labor relations regime was designed to head off the labor militancy through which autoworkers have typically demanded the rising standards of living associated with economic development (Silver 2003). Furthermore, GM's handpicked union ceded to the automaker control of the shop floor, and instead helped manufacture consent for the local version of the GMS. Through these mechanisms, even though workers in Silao experienced the globalization of the North American auto industry as a new economic opportunity rather than the threat felt in Janesville and Arlington, they were subject to the continent-wide decline in the quality of auto work. The broader decline of union power in the United States and Mexico contextualizing labor relations in Janesville, Arlington, and Silao, and the way it unfolded as the North American auto industry globalized, is addressed in the next chapter.

5

Globalization and
Union Decline

The local methods by which GM manufactured consent for the standard-ization and intensification of work along the automaker's assembly lines in Janesville, Arlington, and Silao reflect a broader decline in labor's bargain-ing power as the North American auto industry globalized. This chapter situates each of the labor relations regimes found in those three plants within that trend, as it manifested in each country. In both the United States and Mexico, the institutions through which powerful autoworker unions once made demands of automakers have been undermined as the industry globalized, weakening labor and forcing workers to concede pre-vious gains. This has not only resulted in an intensification of work along the assembly line, but a decline in remuneration as well. These reversals occurred in the United States and Mexico simultaneously, but separately, a common trajectory within the context of each country's national industrial relations system (Katz and Darbishire 2000).

Globalization and National Industrial Relations Systems

Over the last few decades, with the growing economic importance of non-industrial employment, as well as declining union density, there has been a concomitant shift in the study of labor relations. Industrial relations as an interdisciplinary field of inquiry focused predominantly on labor relations between unionized workers and their employers has waned. Scholars studying the employment relationship increasingly do so from their disciplinary homes in economics, sociology, and political science, or perhaps from a "human resources" perspective at a business school. Academic units have renamed themselves as centers for the study of "Employment Relations" and even the Industrial Relations Research Association has been rebranded the Labor and Employment Relations Association.

This academic shift notwithstanding, John Dunlop's (1958) theorization of national industrial relations systems retains explanatory power in understanding the impact of globalization on automotive labor relations—an important industry within industrial relations scholarship. Dunlop theorized national industrial relations systems as involving three actors—labor, management, and government—interacting within a "web of rules" comprised of codified law as well as established practice. Critical to Dunlop's model is the idea that the actors in the industrial relations system, and the system itself, are shaped by, and respond to, the environment in which they are situated. Global economic integration clearly alters the environment in which labor, management, and government interact, forcing each to respond and reweave the web of rules. This reweaving of the rules within countries makes labor relations one of those arenas in which what is commonly perceived as domestic change may actually be attributable to, or at least influenced by, globalization (Sassen 2007).

Wherever a value chain touches down (Bair and Gereffi 2001), therefore, firms encounter and shape local labor relations as actors within these national industrial relations systems. GM's plants in Janesville, Arlington, and Silao are cases in point, with each reflecting the manner in which labor has been weakened as the North American auto industry became globalized. What we see, then, is not identical labor relations from plant to plant, or nation to nation, but a common trajectory as labor became weakened within each country's industrial relations system (Katz and Darbishire 2000).

The following sections tease out this argument by first outlining the national industrial relations systems in the United States and Mexico and how they have developed as the economy has changed. Second, I explain the institutions within each national industrial relations system through which powerful unions negotiated wages and benefits that made autoworkers blue-collar elites in both the United States and Mexico. Then, the impact of globalization on those institutions is analyzed to show how the bargaining power of these unions has been undermined, resulting in a common trajectory of declining pay and intensified labor that has accompanied the globalization of the North American auto industry.

Industrial Relations in the United States

Conceptually, the industrial relations system in the United States reflects a vision of labor relations as a competition between management and labor in which the federal government plays the role of referee. The official rules can be found in two key pieces of federal legislation, the National Labor Relations Act (NLRA) and the Taft-Hartley Act. Passed in 1935, the NLRA granted workers the right to organize and bargain collectively. Also known as the Wagner Act, the NLRA established a National Labor Relations Board (NLRB), a federal agency that oversees union representation votes and otherwise adjudicates disputes between management and labor within its own court system. Under this "New Deal system" (Clawson 2003), collective bargaining was encouraged and workers unionized in droves, particularly in the manufacturing sector. Between 1936 and 1937, union membership skyrocketed from 13.7 to 22.6 percent of nonagricultural workers and then grew steadily for almost a decade, reaching 34.5 percent in 1945 (Goldfield 1989, 10).

This great "upsurge" (Clawson 2003) in union organizing after the passage of the Wagner Act sparked concern among employers and their supporters in Congress, who in 1947 overrode a veto by President Harry Truman to pass the Taft-Hartley Act. Taft-Hartley was intended to readjust the balance of power in labor relations. It weakened unions by placing limitations on strikes, regulating internal union activities, and outlawing "closed shop" agreements that compelled union membership as a condition of employment. The law also allowed states to pass so-called right-to-work laws that ban labor agreements that require workers to pay dues to support the union in their workplace, though unions are legally obligated to represent all workers in a bargaining unit whether or not they are union members.

While reining in unions, Taft-Hartley also empowered employers by strengthening their rights to oppose unions and the organizing efforts of workers. Over the ensuing decades, strategies to prevent workers from organizing unions and to break or weaken unions became well established and widely adopted. Employers honed legal tactics to whittle away support for union organizing, for example by delaying NLRB votes, communicating with workers one-on-one and during mass meetings, and filing endless appeals. Judicial decisions expanded employers' rights, including allowing them to "permanently replace" striking workers even though federal law theoretically protects striking workers from being fired. It also became widespread practice to simply violate U.S. labor law, for example by firing or threatening union supporters, because doing so carries only meager penalties, especially when compared to the effectiveness of such illegal actions in undermining union support and power (Clawson 2003; Goldfield 1989; Gould 2013; Rosenfeld 2014).

By 2013, the share of U.S. workers who were members of unions had dropped to 11.3 percent overall and 6.7 percent in the private sector (U.S. Bureau of Labor Statistics 2014). This was not entirely due to changes in federal labor law and increased employer animus toward unions. Declining employment in traditionally unionized industries and the rise in service sector employment certainly played a role, as did the failure of unions to expand their reach and continue to mobilize as the economy changed (Clawson and Clawson 1999; Kochan 2001). Regardless, there is little doubt that the balance of power in U.S. labor relations has shifted decidedly toward management since the middle of the twentieth century.

Industry-wide Bargaining in the U.S. Auto Industry

Until the globalization of the North American auto industry, U.S. autoworkers were relatively immune to organized labor's decline because the auto industry remained fully unionized. The roots of U.S. automotive labor relations date to the 1937 sit-down strikes, which workers in Janesville supported with a work stoppage of their own. By occupying their plant in Flint, Michigan, workers forced General Motors to recognize their union, which grew into the International Union, United Automobile, Aerospace and Agricultural Implement Workers of America, more commonly known as the United Auto Workers. Unionization at other automakers followed until the industry was nearly completely unionized. Labor-management relations remained hostile until World War II. During the war the automakers and the union declared a labor peace to ensure undisrupted wartime production (though at the local level, strife between management and labor was not so easily quelled).

After the war, concern spread that contentious labor relations would return as the automakers retooled for production of automobiles for the consumer market. Instead, in 1950, Walter Reuther, the head of the UAW, negotiated with General Motors what became known as the "treaty of Detroit," the bedrock of automotive labor relations during the mass production era. Under the agreement, the UAW abandoned its socialist ideology and formally disavowed any demands for control over the means of production or input on business decisions. In exchange, GM agreed, in principle, to guarantee the economic security of its employees and a rising standard of living. Workers would be immunized from the economic consequences of poor managerial decision making (Lichtenstein 1992).

Harry Katz (1985) describes the pillar of U.S. automotive labor relations as industry-wide collective bargaining that removed labor costs as a source of competition among the automakers. By ensuring that wage scales and benefit packages remained comparable among the Detroit automakers, and that similar work was compensated equally within and between the factories of all the companies, the UAW could bargain up wages and benefits without damaging the competitive stature of the firms for whom their members worked. Likewise, since the three major automakers enjoyed an oligopoly in the U.S. market, they could trade higher wages for labor peace, so long as none of the companies gained an advantage in labor costs.

Contract negotiations occurred through a system of "pattern bargaining." As the respective collective bargaining agreements between the UAW and the automakers were expiring, the union would choose one company with which to negotiate. Selecting which to target was a matter of union strategy and depended on which firms were doing well and could best afford generous increases in compensation, or perhaps that could least afford to experience a shutdown due to a strike. The union would then initiate contract negotiations with the so-called strike target. Once the contract was settled, with or without a work stoppage, the UAW then

demanded that the other automakers match the terms that had been negotiated with the strike target.

With wages removed as a source of competition among the automakers,
annual increases became a matter of negotiated formula. Typically, workers received both an annual cost-of-living-adjustment (COLA) pegged to
the inflation rate in addition to a real wage raise of 2 to 3 percent. This real
wage "annual improvement factor" ensured that workers shared the profits
generated by the industry's rising productivity. Combined, these standard
increases guaranteed autoworkers progressively higher real wages, regardless of either short-term fluctuations in the performance of the industry,
their individual employer, or the overall state of the economy.

Along with the annual pay increases, the UAW negotiated an expanding array of benefits for their members, which became an ever-larger percentage of the workers' compensation packages. The UAW's strategy was
to introduce a benefit and then improve it over time. For instance, the
1950 agreement stipulating that the automakers would cover half the cost
of workers' medical insurance eventually grew to full health insurance
coverage. The $100 monthly pension, also introduced in 1950, grew into
a pension system allowing workers to retire after thirty years of service,
regardless of their age. In 1955, the Supplemental Unemployment Benefit
(SUB) was introduced to protect workers during layoffs. SUB pay augmented federal unemployment insurance to ensure workers 65 percent
of their take-home pay for four weeks, and 60 percent for twenty-two
weeks thereafter. By 1967, SUB pay was so comprehensive that laid-off
workers took home 95 percent of their regular pay. Overall, between 1948
and 1980, the cost of benefits rose 1,177 percent, considerably faster than
real wages, which increased an impressive 313 percent (Katz 1985). By the
turn of the twenty-first century, these benefits would be targeted for concessions by the Detroit automakers who saw them as burdensome "legacy
costs" that automakers such as Toyota and Honda did not have to pay
(Rothstein 2008).

In addition to national labor agreements stipulating wages, benefits,
grievance procedures, worker transfer rights, and the overriding governance
structure of labor-management relations, workers were also protected by
the collective bargaining agreements negotiated between local management and union officials discussed in chapter 3. Therefore, labor relations at
each U.S. auto plant were governed by a pair of lengthy, detailed collective
bargaining agreements that specified all the rights and responsibilities of

management and labor and established a process for adjudicating disputes. Under this system, autoworkers in the United States became a privileged group of mostly unskilled blue-collar workers whose steadily increasing real wages set them apart from their counterparts in many other industries. Even as other blue-collar workers saw their buying power decrease as consumer prices rose in the late 1960s and 1970s, autoworkers saw their standard of living continue to improve because their wages kept pace with inflation. By 1980, autoworkers' hourly earnings were 50 percent higher than the average among private sector production workers (Katz 1985).

In many ways, during this Fordist era, automotive labor relations complemented the mass production system based on the Detroit automakers' interpretation of scientific management (Taylor 1911) that called for the complete separation of the conception and execution of work (Crowley et al. 2010). Workers were hired to use their hands, not their minds, and to perform specific tasks as instructed by management. Workers were designated a job among many in a complex classification system. The UAW protected assembly-line workers' rights at work, including guaranteeing that they would not be forced to perform work outside their designated job description. Management was responsible for all business decisions, and had the freedom to determine what products were to be made and how they would be built. In exchange for renouncing any claims to the means of production or input over corporate decision making, the UAW and its members expected and received ever-increasing wages and benefits, regardless of the performance of any particular company.

Mexican Corporatism

The Mexican industrial relations system is rooted in the mechanisms through which a single political party, the Institutional Revolutionary Party (PRI), held on to power and governed the country for most of the twentieth century. The PRI came to power as the National Revolutionary Party in the wake of the 1910 Mexican Revolution that overthrew the dictatorial regime of Porfirio Díaz. In consolidating its power, the National Revolutionary Party sought to incorporate the interests of the various sectors of society that played a part in the revolution, including organized labor. In the 1930s, under the presidency of Lázaro Cárdenas, interest groups were formally incorporated into the ruling party. For organized labor, this meant the establishment of "official unions" with direct ties to, and a voice within, the PRI (Collier and Collier 1991; Middlebrook 1995).

Just as labor was represented within the PRI, so, too, were business groups. This formed the basis of the corporatist industrial relations system in which important decisions affecting labor relations were hashed out within the ruling party. Independently, labor unions in Mexico had little bargaining power with employers. Union membership rates were low, and the nation's level of economic development left a vast pool of unemployed, unskilled labor that undermined the negotiating power of labor unions vis-à-vis management. Unable to demand significant concessions at the bargaining table, organized labor needed a route by which it could achieve its objectives without maintaining a perpetual state of working class mobilization. The corporatist system served that role and established the state as "a privileged arena for resolving disputes between capital and labor" (de la Garza 1994, 196).

However, under the corporatist system, workers' interests were often subsumed within the interests of the PRI. Official unions were meant not only to represent workers but to enforce decisions on them, control the mobilization of workers, and rally support among workers for the PRI at election time. Union leaders who toed the ruling party's line could be rewarded with political patronage. Those who did not could likewise see the mechanisms of power isolate them and their unions.

As a result of the corporatist arrangement, Mexico offers a bit of a paradox. On paper, Mexican workers are granted a wide variety of labor rights that have been difficult for them to exercise in practice. Labor's participation in the Mexican Revolution was rewarded with Article 123 of the 1917 Mexican Constitution, which stipulates that workers have the right to organize unions, collectively bargain, and strike. Article 123 also establishes an array of labor standards that were among the most progressive in the world at the time, and which remain comprehensive to this day. These include an eight-hour day and six-day week, overtime and severance pay, profit sharing, and safety and health provisions (Caulfield 2004).

But the administration of the 1931 Federal Labor Law (FLL) has historically played a larger role than the Constitution in determining to what extent Mexican workers actually realize their constitutional rights. The FLL delegates to state Conciliation and Arbitration Boards (CABs) much of the responsibility for administering labor law, including registering unions and determining whether or not strikes are legitimate or should be declared "nonexistent." In keeping with the corporatist tradition, CABs are tripartite bodies, with representatives from official unions, the government, and business. As a result, workers' pursuing interests that clash with these groups, such as by forming independent unions or engaging in strikes that are counter to government interests or policies, could easily see these efforts squashed. Furthermore, under the FLL, "exclusion clauses" like those found in Silao, whereby workers can be required to be union members as a condition of employment, are legal. In theory, such clauses can strengthen a union in a workplace. But the exclusion clause can also be a tool for keeping workers in line because expulsion from the union also means loss of employment (La Botz 1992; Middlebrook 1995).

In practice, then, though a general direction for labor relations was established at the highest levels of the federal government, there was a great deal of variation geographically and by sector. By far the most powerful unions with the highest membership rolls were official unions, with the largest among these being the CTM. But the country also had notable "independent" unions, for instance at Volkswagen's factory in Puebla, that were not affiliated with the PRI. Furthermore, in the northern state of Nuevo Leon, industrialists in Monterrey established "white unions." Illegal in the United States, and arguably unconstitutional in Mexico (Sanchez 2011), white unions are company unions that are initiated and dominated by firms as a way of controlling workers rather than advancing their interests.

Mexican Automotive Labor Relations during Import Substitution Industrialization

While administering the FLL was left largely to state CABs, the federal government claimed jurisdiction over industrial relations in industries targeted for growth by the PRI as part of its import substitution industrialization (ISI) strategy (Caulfield 2004). ISI policies were designed to grow domestic industry, both through targeted subsidies and by closing the Mexican domestic market to imports. With business and labor each officially represented within the government, the PRI maintained a tenuous national compromise through various forms of cooperation, coercion, and manipulation of Mexico's extensive labor law. The government selected industries targeted for industrialization, including auto, steel, and oil. Employers in these industries enjoyed a captive domestic market and other government protections. Those employers were then expected to pass a portion of their profits on to their employees through wages and benefits. In turn, Mexico's official labor unions with ties to the PRI were responsible for rallying workers in support of the party to which they owed their standard of living. So capital was guaranteed profits. Labor shared in the prosperity. And the PRI maintained its hold on power (Collier and Collier 1991; Middlebrook 1995).

Beginning with the 1962 Automotive Integration Decree requiring all automobiles sold in Mexico to be manufactured domestically, and continuing into the 1980s, the auto industry was targeted for growth (Caulfield 2004), and labor relations in the auto industry facilitated upward mobility among autoworkers. Within the framework of this centralized corporatist system, collective bargaining between unions and employers was highly decentralized, taking place primarily at the plant level. Ford was the only automaker whose employees were all members of the same CTM-affiliated union. Bargaining strategies and levels of labor militancy varied from plant to plant. For instance, workers at GM's facility in Mexico City were consistently more militant than their counterparts forty miles down the road in Toluca (Roxborough 1984; Tuman 1998).

This decentralized bargaining and varying levels of union militancy resulted in broad disparities in wages between plants. By 1980, workers at GM's Mexico City plant earned 52 percent more than their counterparts at the company's Toluca factory, who earned over 30 percent more than autoworkers at Chrysler's and Nissan's Toluca factories. Likewise, the plants differed greatly in the benefit packages workers enjoyed, their approaches to seniority, job classifications, paid leave for union officials, and the degree of control the union enjoyed over the shop floor (Roxborough 1984).

Still, several trends characterized the industry as a whole. First, as a group, autoworkers were among the highest paid blue-collar workers in the country. Second, all the auto plants were unionized closed shops, requiring that every worker be a member of the union. Third, the automakers hired large numbers of temporary workers with less job security or entitlement to compensation during layoffs than regular workers. These temporary workers provided the automakers the flexibility to adjust the size of their workforces during economic downturns without opposition from the unions. Yet, because rank-and-file members were buffered from the employment consequences of economic downturns, they had little reason to moderate their demands when auto sales were slow. Through this system, much like their counterparts in the United States, Mexican autoworkers enjoyed a modicum of job security, steadily increasing standards of living, and considerable input with regard to working conditions on the shop floor (Roxborough 1984).

As in the United States, autoworkers in Mexico became a privileged group of blue-collar workers whose bargaining power stemmed from employment in an industry with a limited number of employers supplying a market with little import penetration. In Mexico, however, the government played a far more active role in two key ways. First, by closing Mexico's domestic market to imports, the PRI's import substitution industrialization strategy allowed domestic automakers to pass rising labor costs along to their customers. Second, the Mexican federal government directly inserted itself into automotive labor relations to ensure the prosperity of autoworkers as the economy expanded more than 7 percent annually (Bensusán and Cook 2003) and, in turn, ensure the political support of those workers and their unions for the ruling party and its policies.

Globalization and the Weakening of Autoworker Unions

For much of the twentieth century, then, the Mexican and U.S. auto industries grew side by side, each manufacturing for its respective domestic market, with little foreign competition. Representing employees of these automotive oligopolies, labor unions in each country negotiated wages and benefits that were the envy of workers in other industries, and work rules that limited managerial prerogative on the shop floor. Though automakers such as GM operated manufacturing facilities in both countries, neither the competition nor their operations were global. Rather, in each country the automakers competed with other firms manufacturing for the domestic market, all of whom participated in an industry-wide labor relations system. In the United States, the three major automakers signed nearly identical collective bargaining agreements that took the cost of labor out of competition. In Mexico, the corporatist state ensured labor's allegiance was rewarded with high wages, benefits, and voice on the factory floor.

Beginning in the late 1970s, however, as these two distinct auto industries consolidated into a single North American auto industry, with an increasing array of automakers assembling and selling vehicles, unions in both countries lost bargaining power. In each country, the foundations of automotive industrial relations through which autoworkers prospered were undermined, weakening unions and ushering in a period of declining wages and benefits, as well as a loss of influence over working conditions along the assembly line. The process by which this occurred in each country reflects their contrasting national industrial relations systems.

The Demise of Industry-wide Pattern Bargaining in the United States

While union density and strength in the United States began steadily declining in the 1950s (Goldfield 1989), for thirty years the UAW and its members were relatively insulated from organized labor's decline. With all three major automakers unionized, autoworkers continued to negotiate higher wages and better benefits packages that further distinguished the industry as one offering good jobs. The globalization of the North American auto industry, however, altered this dynamic as the influx of new automakers from Asia and Europe exposed the UAW to the antilabor environment the rest of the labor movement had faced for decades. By operating nonunion, the so-called transplant assembly factories opened by Japanese, Korean, and German automakers would eventually strike at the heart of the industry-wide pattern bargaining enjoyed by the UAW. With the number of transplants and their workforces expanding as the Detroit automakers contracted, union density in the industry declined, thereby compromising the UAW's capacity to take labor costs out of competition. Over time, the smaller compensation packages paid to autoworkers at the transplant factories led the Detroit automakers to pressure the UAW for concessions in wages and benefits nationally, much as the firms had earlier forced local unions to make concessions on work rules that compromised working conditions.

The earliest transplants owned by Toyota, Honda, and Nissan were careful to prevent union organizing by offering wages comparable to those found in the UAW's contracts with the Detroit automakers (Adler et al. 1997; Mishina 1998). Comparable wages allowed these transplants to counter attempts at unionization by arguing that workers did not need a union to get paid fairly. Benefit and retirement packages were less generous than at the Detroit automakers, however, which kept the overall labor costs at transplant factories lower than those where workers were represented by the UAW. Under these conditions, the UAW lost two union certification votes at Nissan's plant in Tennessee and, due to lack of support, rescinded requests for the NLRB to hold certification votes among workers at Toyota and Honda facilities in Kentucky and Ohio, respectively (Rothstein 2006).

As explained in previous chapters, the earliest effects of the transplants on labor relations in the United States resulted from the competitive urgency they created among the Detroit automakers to implement lean production. In places such as Janesville and Arlington, unions were whipsawed into concessions over work rules and workplace rights so the automakers could gain the flexibility they needed to reorganize work along the assembly line. Rather than complain, local labor leaders adopted a conciliatory tone toward management as the pace of work intensified.

Meanwhile, in national bargaining, the UAW negotiated new contract provisions to protect their members as the Detroit automakers downsized. The length of layoffs was limited. The automakers created "jobs banks" that protected workers who were laid off due to the reorganization of work to implement lean production by paying those workers anyway, a provision of the labor agreement that was widely ridiculed when GM and Chrysler faced bankruptcy (*Automotive News*, January 27, 2014). Workers gained transfer rights in case their plants closed, which led to the creation of the army of so-called GM Gypsies. Still, for the most part, wages and benefits continued to rise for about twenty years, as the Detroit automakers gained cost savings by cutting their workforces but did not directly attack workers' compensation packages (Katz, MacDuffie, and Pil 2002).

Over time, however, as foreign automakers came to realize that they faced little threat of unionization by the UAW, the wages they offered at new facilities fell. For instance, when Toyota opened a plant in San Antonio, Texas, in 2006, starting wages were $15.50 an hour, nearly $10 less than at its Georgetown, Kentucky, facility that opened in 1986 (*Automotive News*, May 14, 2007). In 2008, Honda opened a plant in Greensburg, Indiana, offering wages under $15 an hour, as did Kia in Georgia (*Automotive News*, December 15, 2008). Starting wages at BMW's facility in Spartanburg, South Carolina, were reportedly $14.50 an hour (Brown 2011). Besides paying roughly one half of the wages negotiated by the UAW, none of these plants offered the benefit packages received by unionized autoworkers at the Detroit automakers.

These foreign automakers located in greenfield sites where they could hire workforces with little manufacturing experience and offer them the best new jobs in the area, much as GM did in Silao. And as in Silao, attracting these transplant facilities became a matter of local economic development, with policymakers offering broad financial incentives and infrastructure enhancements to lure automakers (Ruckelshaus and Leberstein 2014). States also emphasized their right-to-work status, and the likelihood of operating nonunion. In Tennessee, where Volkswagen received $577 million in subsidies and tax breaks to open an assembly plant in 2011 that paid workers less than $15 an hour, the governor even openly fought unionization of the plant by conditioning an additional $300 million in state subsidies to expand the facility on the rejection by the workers of the union. The UAW lost the vote 712 to 626, in spite of the fact that Volkswagen, under pressure from German unions, did not fight the organizing drive (*New York Times*, April 4, 2014).

Concession Bargaining in 2007

By 2007, with the average wage differential between union and nonunion autoworkers having grown to 30 percent (Rosenfeld 2014), the UAW could no longer withstand the downward pressure the nonunion auto plants were placing on wages and benefits. In September, not long after I finished fieldwork in Arlington, the UAW and GM negotiated a new collective bargaining agreement in which the union made major concessions in wages, benefits, and work rules. Following the custom of pattern bargaining, workers at Chrysler and Ford ratified similar agreements shortly thereafter. The new agreements included two key provisions, the formation of a voluntary employees' beneficiary association (VEBA) to administer retirees' health insurance and the establishment of a two-tier wage system that would reset starting wages to $14 an hour.

The VEBA is a UAW-run trust fund through which retired automakers receive health insurance. With the creation of the VEBA, the automakers were relieved of their commitment to provide retirees health insurance for life, one of the so-called legacy costs that the nonunion automakers did not have to bear. By 2007, retired union autoworkers outnumbered active UAW members three to one. The VEBA would insulate the automakers from the rising cost of healthcare for a one-time cost of approximately $52 billion. GM, Ford, and Chrysler were to contribute roughly $30, $13.2, and $8.8 billion, respectively (Rothstein 2008). In the wake of GM's 2009 bankruptcy, the VEBA became a major shareholder of the restructured company.

While the VEBA saved the automakers a lot of money, the bigger concession by the UAW was the establishment of a two-tier compensation system. Under the agreement, entry level, "tier two" wages were set at $14 an hour, which was comparable to the starting wage at nonunion transplants and about half as much as more senior, "tier one" workers (Rothstein 2008). Second-tier workers would also enjoy far fewer benefits than their first-tier counterparts (Katz, MacDuffie, and Pil 2013).

In making the deal, the UAW not only accepted a dramatic pay cut for future workers but also put two fundamental principles of industrial unionism in conflict with one another. For seventy years, the UAW held as a matter of principle that workers performing similar work be paid comparably. The union had also fought for strong seniority systems through which older workers segued to easier and more attractive work. Under the two-tier wage system, these policies became incompatible. Either workers on the same assembly line would be paid different rates or the seniority system would be disrupted by carving out separate first- and second-tier jobs.

Implementation would therefore affect working conditions that were traditionally the subject of local collective bargaining. At Ford, it was agreed that newly hired employees would work on the assembly line. This preserved seniority privileges but compromised the concept of equal pay for equal work. By contrast, at GM and Chrysler equal pay for equal work was maintained by assigning new tier-two employees to "noncore" jobs off the assembly line. But in reclassifying those jobs as "noncore," seniority systems were weakened. No longer would older, tier-one workers in places such as Janesville and Arlington eventually move off the assembly line and into those jobs as they aged (Rothstein 2008).

Regardless of the formula they used for implementing the two-tier wage system, the 2007 collective bargaining agreement allowed up to 20 percent of the workforces at the Detroit automakers to work at the second tier. Within months after the agreements were signed, the automakers began offering buyouts to their employees in order to create vacancies to be filled with cheaper labor. GM alone was able to shed up to sixteen thousand tier-one workers, saving the automaker between $4 and $5 billion annually by 2010 (*New York Times*, February 13, 2008). Agreements struck while GM and Chrysler went through bankruptcy proceedings allow those automakers to hire unlimited numbers of second-tier workers. Chrysler has pursued this strategy most aggressively. More than 40 percent their line operators in the United States are now tier-two workers, roughly twice as much as at GM and Ford (*New York Times*, July 15, 2015).

Globalization and Role Reversal in Mexican Unionism

Unlike the steady and gradual decline of the UAW's bargaining power in the United States, union capitulation in Mexico occurred almost overnight as the government dealt with the economic crisis of the early 1980s by embracing the global economy. As oil prices dropped and Mexico found itself without sufficient income to make the interest payments on its foreign debt, the country defaulted on its debt in 1982. The economic structural adjustment policies subsequently forced on the ruling party by the International Monetary Fund, the World Bank, and foreign banks required the PRI to reverse the country's economic course. State-owned industries were privatized. Government spending was slashed. The Mexican peso was devalued, as it would be again in 1995. Import substitution strategies to promote economic development were abandoned in favor of export-oriented industrialization strategies, which quickly segued to neoliberal policy making and an embrace of the global economy (Middlebrook 1995; Schaeffer 2009).

The new economic policies sparked a concomitant shift in industrial relations and the character of unionism in the country. The plant closings that accompanied industrial restructuring eliminated many independent and democratic unions from the manufacturing sector (Bensusán and Cook 2003). At the same time, the government used the corporatist industrial relations system to keep the official unions in line and quell dissent. Whereas the PRI had once encouraged firms in industries protected by ISI policies to raise their workers' pay and benefits, the ruling party instead pressured union officials to make deep concessions on behalf of their members. Even as the country was experiencing double-digit inflation, leaders of Mexico's official labor unions signed national "pacts" limiting pay increases and authorizing management to take steps to promote efficiency and international competitiveness (Bensusán 2000; de la Garza 1998; Grayson 1989).[1] Led by CTM affiliates, of which SITIMM in Silao was typical, increasing numbers of official unions openly embraced the government's economic policies and began espousing a "new union discourse" (Bayón and Bensusán 1998: 128) that eschewed labor militancy in favor of cooperation with management. By 1996, this new approach had been negotiated with employer organizations to establish a "new labor culture" (Caulfield 2004, 459). By behaving in similar fashion to the company-controlled white unions in Monterrey, these official unions sought to gain recognition from employers by making themselves an attractive alternative to the potentially more militant unions that workers might organize on their own. Several human resource managers in Silao indicated they had recognized SITIMM for just this purpose.

In addition, within the rapidly expanding number of factories producing for export, commonly known as *maquiladoras*, ghost unions offering employers protection contracts became prevalent. Although present at only a couple of factories in Silao, ghost unions dominate the *maquiladora* sector. In some regions of Mexico, ghost unions account for the near universal union membership among factory workers (Greer, Stevens, and Stephens 2007; Plankey-Videla 2012). By some estimates, up to 90 percent of all collective bargaining agreements in Mexico are protection contracts (Caulfield 2004). In fact, once workers who are represented by ghost unions are discounted, union membership declined from 30 to 20 percent of the formal labor force between the economic crisis of the early 1980s and the turn of the century (Farris and Levine 2004).

Economic Crisis and Auto Industry Labor Relations

Developments in the auto industry exemplified the shift from manufacturing for the Mexican domestic market to producing cars for export, and eventually integrating into a North American auto industry. Almost overnight, the government urged automakers to manufacture for export and especially to the U.S. market. Doing so was also a competitive imperative for the automakers because the economic crisis and the devaluation of the peso had caused the Mexican automobile market to collapse. But to manufacture for export, the automakers argued, they would need relief from the high pay and stringent work rules that had been negotiated during the ISI era, but which were incompatible with industry efforts to become internationally competitive. Nor could these expenses any longer be passed on to consumers, who were no longer a captive domestic market. If Mexico was to engage the global economy, labor costs would need to be controlled and productivity improved. In response, the leaders of the official unions with deep ties to the PRI agreed to broad concessions across the auto industry that essentially gutted existing collective bargaining agreements.

These concessions by labor leaders, who were unelected by workers themselves, exposed what Enrique de la Garza (1994) describes as a fundamental conflict between the corporatist system, in which business and labor are in partnership with the ruling party, and the increasingly neoliberal direction of the government's policy making. Corporatism assumes a strong interventionist role in the market on behalf of workers; the new policies were designed to cut labor costs. The use of corporatist mechanisms that once benefited autoworkers to instead weaken labor contracts sparked a backlash among the affected rank-and-file autoworkers. Their status as blue-collar elites fading, and their unions no longer providing the economic security to which they had grown accustomed, activists at some auto plants attempted to democratize their unions. Strikes broke out as workers sought to challenge the concessions that were being forced on them, the process by which they were handed down, and to demand reform of the labor movement.

For the most part, these protest movements were thwarted through various governmental, union, and firm maneuvering. For instance, Ford responded to a 1987 strike by workers protesting changes in working conditions by first shutting the plant down, and then reopening the facility with a drastically reduced workforce and a new collective bargaining agreement that ceded to the automaker full control over the production process. There was also occasional violence. By 1993, a new democratic movement surfaced in the same factory, but was again put down, this time in a violent clash on the factory shop floor, during which an activist for union democracy was killed (Carrillo 1995; Garcia and Hills 1998; von Bülow 1998). Similarly, workers at GM's plant in Mexico City struggled for nearly a decade to democratize their union before the company finally closed the plant in 1995 (García and Lara 1998; Micheli 1994) and replaced it with the automaker's new facility in Silao.

In fact, the plant in Silao was part of a trend among automakers looking for more hospitable labor relations environments. In part, automakers in Mexico began opening plants in the northern part of the country to be closer to the new markets in the United States that opened in response to the Mexican government's shift in economic policies and the eventual implementation of NAFTA. But the move was also intended to allow the auto companies to start afresh with new workers and unions in order to escape the union activism in and around the traditional industrial heartland (Micheli 1994). Since collective bargaining in the Mexican auto industry had always been decentralized (Roxborough 1984), it became a matter of finding the right bargaining partner. In opening their new plants, the automakers increasingly recognized unions affiliated with the CTM because of its support for the government's economic policies and assistance in protecting the automakers from union militancy. In addition, collective bargaining was reformed to focus nearly exclusively on remuneration, as it was in Silao. Unlike during the ISI era, automakers were ceded near complete control over the shop floor, free to organize work to implement lean production or other productivity enhancing manufacturing techniques (Bayón and Bensusán 1998; Micheli 1994).

So in Mexico, the decline in compensation and widespread adoption of lean production was facilitated by the manipulations of the corporatist system through which the ruling party convinced the official labor movement to renounce their previous labor agreements. In Mexico's industrial heartland in and around Mexico City, this meant allowing the automakers to regain control of the shop floor by fiat and, if necessary, by force. In more northern regions of the country, the automakers borrowed a page from the transplants operating in the United States. They opened greenfield sites like that in Silao and socialized new workers to lean production from the outset, with the aid of compliant labor organizations.

It is difficult to calculate the exact loss of income autoworkers have experienced as a result of the national pacts limiting pay increases, the peso devaluations in 1982 and 1995, and the systematic weakening of unions as the North American auto industry globalized. But the 1995 peso devaluation alone cut real wages in the automotive sector in half, to 18 percent of the wages earned by autoworkers in the United States employed by many of the same automakers. By 2002, real wages in the non-*maquiladora* sector were 8 percent lower than they had been in 1994, in spite of productivity increases of almost 45 percent (Caulfield 2004).

Labor Relations after the PRI

In 2000, Vicente Fox Quesada of the National Action Party (PAN) became president of Mexico, marking the end of the PRI's hold on the position it had held since the Mexican Revolution. In fact, the PRI had been losing its grip on power at the state and legislative level for some time. From 1995 to 1999, Fox himself had served as governor of the state of Guanajuato, where GM's Silao plant is located. Yet, given the power that Mexican presidents have traditionally yielded, the PRI's loss was considered a significant step toward a more democratic Mexico (La Botz 2005).

With the election of Fox, the fate of what remained of the corporatist industrial relations system and Mexico's official unions became a subject of open debate (Bensusán and Cook 2003). If the PRI was no longer in power, there were no longer official unions with ties to the governing party. In reality, the corporatist system had frayed over the previous fifteen years, and likely contributed to the PRI's loss of power. As the PRI shifted Mexico's economic policies away from ISI to embrace a more neoliberal agenda, some leaders among the official unions objected. Those who supported the party often found that they were unable to reliably deliver the votes of workers as they had before. So labor lost clout in the PRI, which eventually could not muster a voting majority (Bensusán 2004). By 2000, a number of labor unions had broken away from the PRI to form an independent labor confederation, the National Union of Workers.

Fox's assumption of the presidency was also seen by some as an opportunity to reform Mexican labor law. Two different sets of labor law reform were proposed. Business groups and their allies sought to "modernize" Mexican labor law to create greater labor market flexibility, by loosening labor standards to allow employers to hire part-time and temporary workers and to contract out work. Labor activists, on the other hand, wanted to revise Mexican labor law to promote union democracy and the spread of independent unions. Their proposal included reforming the CABs and the union exclusion clause, outlawing ghost unions, and safeguarding union members' rights. Neither proposal garnered sufficient political support to pass the legislature, and neither was strongly advocated by Fox (Caulfield 2004; Greer, Stevens, and Stephens 2007).

Instead, Mexican industrial relations have mostly followed the trajectory set forth with the embrace of globalization in the mid-1980s. Ghost unions have proliferated in the *maquiladora* sector, becoming ubiquitous in parts of the country. CTM unions, such as SITIMM in Silao, offer employers a more active, but nonmilitant, alternative to ghost unions. White unions continue to be prevalent in Monterrey. And the country maintains a fledgling independent union movement that does not represent a lot of workers in the private sector and poses little real threat to business interests in the country. It does, however, fill a political void advocating labor issues (Bensusán 2004).

De-unionization and Declining Job Quality in the North American Auto Industry

For several decades after World War II, in both the United States and Mexico, the national industrial relations system promoted collective bargaining. Workers were encouraged to form and join unions. In each country's auto industry, powerful unions negotiated for autoworkers the wages, benefits, and working conditions that made them the envy of other blue-collar workers. In the United States, industry-wide pattern bargaining between the UAW and the Detroit automakers that dominated the domestic market facilitated rising standards of living by taking labor costs out of competition. At each auto plant, where plant managers were under pressure to maintain production to meet increasing demand for vehicles, local unions negotiated an expansive array of work rules and exercised a degree of control over the shop floor in exchange for keeping the assembly line moving. In Mexico, through the corporatist industrial relations system, the ruling party ensured that automakers negotiated with labor unions to increase autoworkers' standards of living and improve working conditions, the costs of which could be passed on to consumers through the ISI strategies that closed the domestic market to imports.

As the North American auto industry globalized, that all changed. In the United States, the experiences of workers in Janesville and Arlington reflect an overall trend of declining union density and bargaining power, and a resulting drop in remuneration and working conditions. Between 1982 and 2011, Japanese, German, and Korean automakers opened seventeen auto assembly plants in the United States, all operating union free. They employ nearly sixty thousand workers, or roughly 30 percent of automotive production workers in the United States (Katz, MacDuffie, and Pil 2013). By paying lower wages and benefits, these automakers put labor costs back into competition, ultimately forcing the UAW to concede wages and benefits cuts to the Detroit automakers. Between 2003, when research for this book began, and 2013 alone, real wages among motor vehicle assembly workers in the United States declined over 20 percent (Katz, MacDuffie, and Pil 2013; Ruckelshaus and Leberstein 2014).

In Mexico, weakening labor, cutting pay and benefits, and returning control of production to management became explicit policy as the government sought to promote exports and join the global economy. The very corporatist arrangement through which labor had prospered under ISI became a tool for forcing concessions and suppressing wages as official unions become partners in the drive to increase efficiency to promote manufacture for export. In both countries, through mechanisms as different as their national industrial relations systems, wages and benefits fell while union influence over the shop floor and ability to regulate working conditions waned. And in both countries, the unions representing autoworkers adopted a conciliatory language toward the automakers as they sought to "partner" with them to remain competitive.

So in both the United States and Mexico, job quality in the auto industry has declined as the globalization of the North American auto industry undermined the labor relations institutions through which workers in each country once negotiated increases in wages and benefits and improvements in working conditions. Could it have been otherwise, and how? Could the auto industries of North American have integrated, welcomed competition and transplants from Asia and Europe, and adopted the best practices of lean production without compromising wages, benefits, and working conditions? This is the question that will be addressed in the conclusion.

6

Conclusion

Toward a Better-Regulated
Global Economy

"It's not looking very good for the union auto worker right now." Thus concluded an e-mail I received from a GM employee in 2008. Middle-aged, with a family to support, he had lived and worked through the globalization of the North American auto industry. He had seen GM lose market share and his union lose clout. He had experienced plant closures, concessions in wages and benefits, and an intensification of his labor. Now, his most recent workplace was shutting down, leaving him pondering whether to move, yet again, in order to maintain employment with GM. The automaker still offered the best jobs around, even if the quality of those jobs had declined.

He had no idea what was just on the horizon. The worldwide financial crisis hit later that year. In 2009, the hundred-year-old automaker declared bankruptcy and reorganized under the guidance of the Obama administration's Auto Industry Taskforce. The "New GM" emerged smaller and leaner. A third of its six thousand dealerships closed (*New York Times*, July 18, 2010), as did a dozen factories. The workforce was reduced by 20,000. The storied Pontiac nameplate passed into history. Saturn, the brand that had been introduced with fanfare in the 1980s as a "different kind of car company," was also eliminated. The Hummer line of SUVs, modeled on military vehicles, was discontinued after plans to sell the division to a Chinese company fell through. Saab, the Swedish brand with shrinking sales that GM had owned for less than a decade, was sold off. That left the "New GM" selling cars in the United States under four brands: Chevrolet, GMC, Buick, and Cadillac (*New York Times*, February 16, 2009).

Ownership of the New GM was split between the "old" GM's creditors, the UAW health-care trust fund, and the U.S. federal government. U.S. taxpayers held a 60 percent stake after pouring $30 billion into the company, in addition to the almost $20 billion the outgoing Bush administration had lent the automaker in a failed attempt to stave off bankruptcy (*New York Times*, June 30, 2009). The plan was for the government to divest itself of company stock slowly, once the automaker was again ready to be publicly traded. Renewed profitability, the public was told, would come as GM diversified its products to include more fuel efficient and alternative-fueled vehicles, and fewer SUVs like the ones made in Janesville, Arlington, and Silao. In 2010, the automaker reported a $4.7 billion profit (*New York Times*, June 30, 2009), allowing the government to begin selling its stock earlier than had been projected (*New York Times*, November 17, 2010). By the end of 2013, the U.S. government officially ended its role in the bailout by selling its remaining stock in the automaker (*New York Times*, December 9, 2013).

Still, GM's return to profitability did not eliminate the dilemma faced by autoworkers. The U.S. auto industry has not experienced just a competitive downturn. Rather, the entire North American auto industry has undergone a process of globalization that has shifted the balance of power in the industry's labor relations. Historically, workers and their labor unions had leverage to demand higher wages and benefits and a modicum of control over the shop floor. As a result, the auto industry has long been associated with "good" jobs that pay well and offer ample benefits and decent working conditions. In mature economies like that of the United States, the autoworker became emblematic of the rise of a blue-collar middle class in the twentieth century. For countries such as Mexico, the growth of an automotive sector offered hope for stable, well-remunerated employment, and broader economic development (Silver 2003).

But in the global economy this appears not necessarily to be the case. As the U.S.-Canadian and Mexican auto industries integrated into a single, continent-wide, North American auto industry with a host of new automakers that prompted an industrial restructuring from mass production to lean production, autoworkers have become relatively worse off. This process of globalization has undermined organized labor and the labor relations institutions through which autoworkers once gained wages, benefits, and working conditions that made them blue-collar elites. As a result, auto industry pay has declined, benefits have been scaled back, and the pace of work has intensified.

In the United States, the rise of a large, nonunion automotive sector became a slow drag on wages and benefits throughout the industry. Initially, the union avoidance strategies of the foreign transplants included matching the union pay scale. Over time, however, nonunion pay dropped—almost in half. This led to deep concessions within the unionized sector, including the establishment of two-tier wage system under which the entry-level wage at the Detroit automakers was cut in half and benefits slashed (Katz, MacDuffie, and Pil 2013; Rosenfeld 2014; Rothstein 2008). Likewise, the introduction of lean production by the transplants operated by foreign automakers, absent any union presence to negotiate and uphold working conditions, led to the whipsawing of unionized auto plants in places such as Janesville and Arlington. The resulting concessions in workplace rights and work rules allowed the Detroit automakers to intensify work on the assembly line. Instead of workers in the transplants becoming militant, organizing, and demanding higher remuneration and greater control over the production process, the UAW has been weakened and become increasingly conciliatory toward management.

The globalization of the North American auto industry has had similar effects on Mexican autoworkers, but through a different dynamic. In Mexico, where for almost forty years after World War II the auto industry grew under the protection of government policies to achieve import substitution industrialization, globalization meant the sudden abandonment of ISI and a shift to automotive production for export. Without a protected domestic market to which labor costs could be passed on, automakers in Mexico demanded and received cuts in wages and benefits, as well as renewed control over work on the shop floor (Bensusán 2000; de la Garza 1998; Grayson 1989). When workers rebelled against the concessions made by leaders of the country's official unions, automakers began moving away from militant workers in the industrial heartland around Mexico City, heading north to establish new plants in greenfield sites (Micheli 1994). Similar to the new transplants in the United States, these Mexican greenfield sites in places like Silao allowed automakers to offer lower wages and implement lean production without union interference or militancy (Bayón and Bensusán 1998), among inexperienced workforces grateful for a life-altering economic opportunity. Consequently, in Mexico as in the United States, globalization has compromised job quality as wages and benefits have declined and the pace of work has intensified.

In both the United States and Mexico, globalization has prompted a race to the bottom in auto industry labor standards. To be sure, it is a race to the bottom quite different than that found in the garment industry and other buyer-driven value chains (Gereffi 1994). In the North American auto industry, the race is not among poor countries vying for jobs in low-wage, low-value-added manufacturing. Instead, this is a competition for relatively high-wage, high-value-added manufacturing, being fought among localities within, not necessarily between, the two countries. Similar to the competition among low-wage countries desperate to attract even sweatshop factories, the winners of new assembly plants and jobs in the auto industry are those willing to compromise their labor rights and standards. This race to the bottom may be more of a marathon, with wages, benefits, workplace rights, and labor standards being slowly eroded, but the trajectory is clear. Even these good jobs are getting worse.

At the heart of this race to the bottom lies the failure of the respective national industrial relations systems in the United States and Mexico to maintain labor's bargaining leverage as the North American auto industry underwent a process of globalization. In the United States, for a variety of reasons, organized labor has experienced a steady decline in union membership and collective bargaining power since the 1950s (Burns 2011; Clawson 2003; Clawson and Clawson 1999; Goldfield 1989; Kochan, Katz, and McKersie 1994; Nissen 2003). This decline in unions has contributed to a widening chasm between good skilled jobs and bad unskilled jobs, as the latter became ever less unionized (Kalleberg 2011). For decades, industry-wide collective bargaining between the UAW and Detroit automakers insulated autoworkers from the consequences of labor's declining influence nationally. However, as the North American auto industry globalized, autoworkers became exposed to the consequences of labor's declining leverage in U.S. labor relations. In particular, the UAW found itself confronting the union avoidance strategies, both legal and illegal, honed by management over years, which had severely hindered labor's capacity to organize (Clawson and Clawson 1999; Goldfield 1989; Rosenfeld 2014). With the UAW unable to organize workers at the foreign transplants, the industry-wide collective bargaining that had brought autoworkers into the middle class began to fray. No longer able to keep labor costs from becoming a source of competition between automakers, the UAW began making concessions to the Detroit automakers in order to keep them competitive with the nonunion sector (Katz, MacDuffie, and Pil 2013; Rosenfeld 2014; Rothstein 2006, 2008).

In Mexico, the economic crisis of the early 1980s, which precipitated the embrace of economic policies that would facilitate the globalization of the North American auto industry, struck directly at the heart of labor's power. Before this shift, the Mexican federal government had been labor's benefactor in the corporatist industrial relations system. Labor's power emanated from its relationship with and within the ruling PRI (Collier and Collier 1991; Middlebrook 1995). Under ISI policies, the government could persuade automakers to share with their workers the profits that were generated in a market that lacked foreign competition. With the abandonment of ISI and the move toward neoliberal economic policies at the behest of international creditors, however, the ruling party used its power over the country's unions to gain concessions that automakers claimed were necessary to become internationally competitive. Almost overnight, the bargaining leverage that autoworkers once enjoyed disappeared as the CTM unions that dominate the auto industry adopted a philosophy of labor-management cooperation as a strategy for gaining recognition from automakers (Bayón and Bensusán 1998; Caulfield 2004).

A German Counterexample

Particularly for those who imagine globalization as an inexorable force (Friedman 2005), it may be tempting to view the declining quality of auto work in the United States and Mexico as an unfortunate, but unavoidable, consequence of globalization, perhaps even a competitive imperative. But the case of German autoworkers offers a telling comparison. Including pay and benefits, German autoworkers earn roughly twice that of U.S. autoworkers, some of whom work for the same German automakers, namely

Volkswagen, Mercedes, and BMW. Apparently, this has not crippled the competitiveness of German assembly plants. Germany produces roughly twice as many automobiles as the United States annually (Brown 2011).

It is not that German autoworkers have been immune to globalization. Germany is part of the European Union (EU), a far more expansive integration of economies than was attempted by the signatories to NAFTA (Kaminska 2013). In fact, the expansion of the EU to include eastern European countries prompted fears that capital flight to low-wage countries, or "social dumping," would spark a race to the bottom (Krzywdzinski 2014). Within the EU, competition among automakers, including those from Detroit, is intense. The industry has been influenced by the industrial restructuring and reorganization of work associated with lean production (Boyer et al. 1998; Kochan, Lansbury, and MacDuffie 1997). So why have German autoworkers apparently fared so much better than their counterparts in North America, some of whom work for the same automakers?

Unlike in the United States and Mexico, auto industry labor relations have not been substantially undermined in Germany. To the contrary, efforts have been made to shore up the country's national industrial relations system in the face of globalization. German law provides for industry-wide collective bargaining and the workers' right to a "works council" through which management and labor dialogue over issues that affect job quality, from scheduling to shop floor conditions. As a result, in the German auto industry collective bargaining is vaguely reminiscent of the pre-globalization era in the U.S. industry. Industry-wide collective bargaining between the union IG Metal and the automakers takes labor out of competition, much as the UAW was once able to do by negotiating with the Detroit automakers. Factory-level bargaining occurs through the works councils, much as local affiliates of the UAW negotiate with GM, Ford, and Chrysler plant managers (Behrens 2013).

These German policies promoting collective bargaining were somewhat protected in the negotiation of the agreements forming the European Union. German policymakers and their European colleagues incorporated a Social Charter within the European Union. The Social Charter includes "directives" promoting health and safety standards and banning sex discrimination in the workplace, as well as a range of labor law over issues such as work hours, part-time work, and so forth. Negotiations over directives include recognized representatives of European labor and management referred to as the "social partners." Directives do not create European-wide law, but through "subsidiarity" instead obligate members to augment their own national laws to incorporate EU directives (Due, Madsen, and Jensen 1991). So while states within the EU maintain their unique industrial relations systems, the EU has layered a continental system of industrial relations, complete with designated actors, for developing some universal labor standards and practices that each state incorporates into its own web of rules.

Among these directives is the European Works Councils Directive originally passed in 1994 and updated in 2009. The directive requires all members of the EU to facilitate the formation of works councils at any firm with more than 1,000 employees in the EU and more than 150 employees in at least two countries. The explicit purpose of the works councils is for management to provide workers' representatives with information regarding the business and to consult with them over business decisions. While not ordering collective bargaining, the European Works Councils Directive clearly establishes workers' rights to information that could be used in collective bargaining, with the understanding that such information will be shared among works councils and unions throughout the EU (Behrens 2013; Kaminska 2013).

The North American Agreement for Labor Cooperation

By comparison, negotiations between Mexican, Canadian, and U.S. policymakers over concerns about the impact that NAFTA might have on labor produced a much weaker North American Agreement for Labor Cooperation (NAALC). Unlike the European Social Charter, the NAALC explicitly renounces the idea that labor relations in North American should include any continent-wide web of rules to which the countries should adhere. Rather, "recognizing the right of each Party to establish its own domestic labor standards" (NAALC, Article 2) and maintaining "due regard for the economic, social, cultural and legislative differences between them" (NAALC, Article 11(3)), the NAALC outlines eleven "principles" that Mexico, Canada, and the United States agree to promote cooperatively. These eleven principles include freedom of association and the right to organize; the right to bargain collectively; the right to strike; prohibition of forced labor; labor protections for children; minimum employment standards; elimination of employment discrimination;

equal pay for men and women; prevention of occupational injuries and illnesses; compensation for occupational injuries, and the protection of migrant workers. However, the NAALC leaves to each country the right to define what these principles mean and determine how they should be implemented and enforced.

Essentially, the NAALC recommitted each country to enforcing its own labor laws and established a Commission for Labor Cooperation to organize joint activities to promote labor standards. In this spirit of cooperation, the NAALC lacks any enforcement mechanism. Instead, each country has a National Administrative Office (NAO) to which complaints can be brought alleging that the labor law in another country is not being enforced. Such submissions trigger an investigative process through which the NAO determines whether or not officials in another country are enforcing its labor law. While these NAO findings can ultimately trigger consultations between the governments over the issues, there is no mechanism to compel enforcement. In fact, there is nothing in the NAALC that prevents a country from changing its laws to weaken labor standards (Kaminska 2013).

In spite of some early enthusiasm that the NAALC might offer a unique means of addressing labor issues in North America (Compa 1995), it is difficult to see where the agreement has had any effective impact on labor standards in any country. Perhaps the best that can be said about the NAALC is that it encourages cross-border relationships and collaborations between labor activists (Kay 2005). Ultimately, however, the NAALC, by its very existence, is a tacit recognition that economic integration has some potentially deleterious impacts on labor, but does little to prevent or address such outcomes.

Contrasting Approaches to Globalization

Admittedly, one should not go too far in comparing the European Union to NAFTA. The EU is far more comprehensive, incorporating not only the economic integration of Europe's economies but an explicit political component as well. The European Commission is a continent-wide policy-making body that sometimes speaks internationally for its members. By contrast, NAFTA is merely a trade agreement that opens North American borders to the flow of goods, and to a lesser extent services

(Kaminska 2013). On the other hand, the broad differences between the EU and NAFTA are exactly the point. They offer a reminder of the shear breadth of approaches possible in addressing the industrial relations web of rules within the global economy.

Without suggesting that the EU Social Charter offers full protection for European workers, it is fair to say that the European approach to globalization exhibits a concerted effort to anticipate and address potential threats to labor posed by the formation of the EU. By contrast, negotiations over the NAALC failed to address the undermining of labor already under way within each country's industrial relations system. By the time the NAALC was being negotiated in 1993, the failure of U.S. labor law to protect workers' rights to organize unions and bargain collectively was well documented. In Mexico, the fallout of the 1980s economic crisis and the manner in which the country's official unions renounced protections for workers and facilitated declining wages and workplace protections through the spread of conciliatory unions and ghost unions was well established.

Perhaps workers in both countries might have fared better under a NAALC designed to shore up collective bargaining in North America rather than merely affirm workers' basic rights without any mechanism for guaranteeing them. Perhaps had the foreign transplant assembly plants in the United States been unionized, the wages of U.S. autoworkers would not have fallen, or at least not as much. Perhaps the intensification of work along the assembly line as automakers implemented lean production might have been ameliorated by greater union strength in the plants and on the shop floor, if Detroit automakers were not whipsawing local unions to match conditions in nonunion plants. Similarly, it is not difficult to imagine that Mexican autoworkers might have weathered the country's economic storm better had their rights to organize and collectively bargain been protected rather than undermined. This is certainly true for the autoworkers who experienced Mexico's shift to production for export and fought to democratize their unions, some of whom lost their jobs altogether as the automakers relocated to greenfield sites like Silao. But even in places such as Silao, where workers celebrate their good fortune for landing a job with GM, workers might benefit from unions they form themselves rather than those selected by their employers, which look the other way even as firms undermine collective bargaining by conspiring among themselves to fix the local labor market.

However, the NAALC was never intended to address, much less rectify, labor's declining influence in each country. NAFTA was originally negotiated without any mention of labor. It was only as a result of pressure by organized labor in the United States on Bill Clinton when he was running for president that the idea of a labor side agreement to NAFTA was born. Clinton was running to unseat President George H. W. Bush, whose administration had negotiated NAFTA. Also running as an independent was H. Ross Perot, whose campaign centered on his opposition to NAFTA, and the tremendous job loss he said it would cause in the United States as employers fled to low-wage Mexico. To appease key Democratic constituencies and stake out a middle ground, Clinton supported NAFTA on the condition that additional side agreements would be negotiated to address labor and environmental issues. Once elected, Clinton managed to get Congress to approve NAFTA over organized labor's objections that the labor side agreement was toothless. So while the European Social Charter was integral to the formation of the EU, the NAALC was quite literally an afterthought in the creation of NAFTA.

Toward Strengthened International Labor Standards

The type of transnational labor regulations that are needed to shore up collective bargaining and prevent the race to the bottom in the auto industry are far more extensive than commonly proposed measures to counter sweatshops and other blatant abuses of workers. Often, efforts to end sweatshops revolve around consumer-based campaigns that circumvent national industrial relations systems altogether. Instead, by focusing on the dynamics of buyer-driven commodity chains (Gereffi 1994) in which retailers dictate to their offshore manufacturers the quality standards and prices for goods, activists seek to pressure retailers to include higher labor standards in the demands they place on their suppliers. Sweatshop activists have launched high-profile campaigns designed to force companies such as Nike, the GAP, Disney, and Starbucks to take responsibility for, and assert control over, the labor standards under which their products are produced. Along similar lines, organizations such as Students Against Sweatshops have lobbied their universities to force the licensees of their logos to certify, through independent monitoring, the labor standards at the factories where the clothes are manufactured (Featherstone 2002). These movements and ones like them have helped develop certification standards by which consumer goods can be labeled "fair trade." It has been even been suggested that, in theory at least, sufficient interest by consumers could create a dynamic in which labor standards "ratchet up" as consumers demand ever better treatment of workers (Fung, O'Rourke, and Sabel 2001).

Doubts about the efficacy of codes of conduct beyond those firms dedicated to maintaining decent working conditions aside (Seidman 2007), the scope of such efforts is quite limited. They only apply to goods with fairly straightforward value chains and sufficient alternatives that conscientious consumers can reasonably be expected to select a product based, at least in part, on the labor conditions under which it was produced. This may work for T-shirts, but it is difficult to imagine someone deciding which SUV to drive based on the labor conditions at a wire harness factory in Silao, Mexico. Furthermore, codes of conduct do little to establish and support industrial relations systems that promote workers' ability to organize their own unions, demand their own rights, and improve their own working conditions in the absence of pressure from consumers in other parts of the world. Nor do these campaigns advance labor rights and standards for all workers in the global economy, just those producing for export those certain items around which consumers can be rallied and encouraged to pay a little more to ensure decent working conditions.

Public policy proposals to address labor standards in the global economy often suffer from similar limitations in scope by attempting to rectify only the most egregious violations of basic worker rights where goods for the consumer market are produced. For instance, the International Labor Organization's (ILO) Declaration on Fundamental Principles and Rights at Work (1998) seeks only to secure the most basic of worker rights by focusing on eight ILO conventions. If adhered to, these eight conventions would eliminate all forms of forced or compulsory labor, abolish child labor, eliminate discrimination in employment and occupation, and ensure the freedom of association and the right to collective bargaining—perhaps the minimum required to address the sweatshop issue.

In fact, the Declaration on Fundamental Principles and Rights at Work can be interpreted as ILO backtracking in an effort to regain relevancy. The ILO has been codifying labor rights and standards since its inception in 1919. In addition to its "core labor standards," the ILO's 188 conventions also address an array of topics including, but not limited to, minimum wages, work hours and paid time off, unemployment insurance and social security, and job security. Of course, though ILO conventions have been widely ratified by countries around the world, they are also routinely violated. Lacking any mechanism for enforcing conventions, the Fundamental Principles appear to be the ILO's effort to at least harness its moral authority to shine a light on the most egregious labor abuses in the global economy.

Actually making a dent in the sweatshop problem would be a tremendous victory for workers. Yet doing so would still fall well short of what is necessary to advance the cause of labor in the global economy. As the cases in this book exemplify, the impact of globalization on workers is pervasive, undermining labor in rich and poor countries alike across a host of industries. Many jobs are affected by globalization without workers becoming sweatshop laborers. Addressing these broader ramifications of a globalizing economy requires a transnational industrial relations web of rules that shores up existing, and encourages the development of, national labor relations systems that uphold worker rights and labor's capacity to bargain collectively with management.

No doubt, advancing a global economy that encourages states to protect and promote worker rights to organize and collectively bargain is a monumental task and long-term struggle. The European Union and its Social Charter were negotiated and implemented over decades among democratic countries with relatively similar standards of living. Indeed, incorporating into the global economic regulatory infrastructure provisions that empower workers to exercise labor rights within their respective national industrial relations systems will require imagining and realizing an alternative model of globalization that addresses labor issues at its core rather than treats them as a peripheral issue.

The Political Economy of Globalization

In the Introduction, economic globalization is conceptualized as the increasing interconnectedness and integration of economies, due to international agreements to expand trade and investment. Globalization is, therefore, the result of a political agenda articulated within details of international agreements and agencies (McMichael 2008; Sassen 2007), be it the World Trade Organization, the European Union, or NAFTA. This understanding of the global economy stands in contrast to the popular notion that globalization is some nebulous force unleashed by advances in technology and communications that one can attempt to take advantage of, but not control (Friedman 2005). There is no doubt that many of the autoworkers with whom I spoke experienced globalization as an uncontrollable force, whether they had experienced threats to their livelihoods in Janesville and Arlington or gotten new jobs in Silao. But this vision of globalization overlooks the myriad domestic and international policies designed to integrate the United States, Canadian, and Mexican economies, and increase competition within North America, which precipitated the restructuring of the North American auto industry. So globalization may prompt change that feels uncontrollable on the ground, but it is the result of decisions over how to regulate, and what not to regulate effectively, in the global economy.

The general trajectory of the policies promoting and governing globalization are often characterized as "neoliberal" for their general tilt toward reducing barriers to trade and deregulating markets. In popular parlance, neoliberalism is the language of "free markets" and "free trade" that have become effective marketing terms for selling policies associated with globalization (Clawson 2003). Identifying the global economy with neoliberalism provides a common reference point for critiquing the global economy and suggests the possibility of a counterhegemonic movement to fix many of the problems with globalization, from labor to the environment and beyond (Evans 2008). Indeed, the growing concern for international labor rights and standards, as well as increasing transnational labor cooperation and activism, are sometimes seen as labor's embrace of globalization to address and combat the consequences of neoliberal polices on workers (Bronfenbrenner 2007; Clawson 2003; Gordon and Turner 2000; Webster, Lambert, and Bezuidenhout 2008).

The downside to this formulation is that the global economy is not a manifestation of neoliberal economic theory put into practice. The global economy is replete with violations of neoliberalism (Evans 2008). This study is a case in point. In a neoliberal economy, GM would have been allowed to disappear into bankruptcy in 2008. The automaker owes its continued existence to government intervention in the market by both the Bush and Obama administrations. Moreover, the $50 billion it cost to bail out GM was diverted from the $700 billion Troubled Asset Relief

Program, a massive federal intervention to stabilize financial markets and stave off a global depression, which clearly violated neoliberal principles.

Even in areas where national economic policies might appear to embrace neoliberalism, this has only resulted in the delegation of development policy making to local and regional officials. There is rarely an auto plant constructed in North America without the automaker's shopping around for state and local government subsidies of some sort, like those GM received in Silao and which European and Asian automakers have enjoyed in the United States. In places like Janesville and Arlington, Detroit's automakers have also extracted subsidies, tax breaks, and other promises from state and local governments desperate to keep their local plants and the good jobs they offer. The automakers and these regional officials are not adhering to neoliberal economics.

To be sure, neoliberal arguments dominate the opposition to securing or raising labor standards through international agreements, to promoting unions and collective bargaining, and even to raising the minimum wage. From a neoliberal perspective, even if well intentioned, such measures are market distorting and result in suboptimum economic outcomes that may ultimately harm workers whose best interest lies in expanding the economy. Yet concerns for the preservation of free labor markets do not prompt action in the more rare occasions when the market distortions result in artificially lower labor costs. China's inclusion in the WTO came in spite of, and without addressing, policies that frequently limit worker mobility, the very freedom to seek employment freely and to change jobs that should be at the heart of any neoliberal labor market (Lee 2007; Schaeffer 2009). Similarly, no government officials stepped in to disrupt the local labor relations regime that GM orchestrated among its suppliers in Silao, which was designed to restrain wages and interfere with workers' rights freely to sell their labor, in clear violation of neoliberal principles and Mexican labor law as well.

Upon even this cursory examination, it is obvious that the global economy is not a neoliberal order. Instead, what we see in these policies and those regulating the global economy is the implementation of political settlements that reflect a business agenda. Often, the very bilateral and multilateral agreements to reduce barriers to trade while protecting intellectual property rights are negotiated behind closed doors with business interests in mind (McMichael 2008; Schaeffer 2009). Without a doubt, this business agenda frequently parallels neoliberal theory, and the rhetoric of neoliberalism is certainly prevalent. But neoliberal principles are just as easily abandoned when they are incompatible with, or might be an obstacle to, an agreement taking shape.

Once the global economy is understood as the manifestation of political settlements rather than neoliberal economics, what might otherwise appear as contradictory approaches to markets, to trade, to subsides, and to labor become consistent because they all seek to advance some empowered interest. Only in this light is it not inconsistent for policymakers simultaneously to intervene in the market by offering incentives to lure auto plants to specific states while arguing that unions violate the sanctity of the free market. Similarly, though a neoliberal agenda in Mexico would have led to a weakening of labor in favor of unregulated labor markets, neoliberalism would not include government-promoted unions that permit GM and its suppliers to price fix the cost of labor and divvy up the labor market as they do in Silao.

Distinguishing between neoliberalism and the actual policies behind the globalization project has important implications. Critiquing the global economy as neoliberalism not only misses the mark but also inadvertently provides the cover of economic theory to current policies shaping globalization, rather than exposing the political and economic interests behind that policy making. The problem is not that the neoliberal economy is bad for workers, but that the interests of workers do not get equal footing to those of business when it comes to structuring and regulating the global economy.

So the dilemma for labor is not a dominant economic policy, but the political power of capital in shaping the global economy. The evidence is in the content of actual international agreements. Where labor is at its most politically powerful, in Europe, negotiations over the formation and governance of the European Union provided labor a seat at the table and included provisions addressing labor's concerns. In North America, the NAALC reflects labor's relative weakness in comparison to its European counterparts. Labor in the United States was politically strong enough to force presidential candidate Bill Clinton to promise a labor side agreement to NAFTA. But once he was elected labor was too weak to ensure negotiation of an agreement that would protect workers' interests or to prevent NAFTA from being ratified over organized labor's objections. In the global economy, labor has far too little power to even warrant recognition by the

World Trade Organization. As a result, the WTO not only fails to address labor issues but also includes countries that forbid workers from organizing themselves politically or within the workplace at all.

Understanding the institutions that constitute the global economic infrastructure as reflecting a political balance of power rather than the policy manifestation of neoliberal economics provides some guidance for the future. Labor unions and activists need to build support for an alternative globalization that promotes economic growth and development not by forsaking labor rights and standards but by expanding them. Admittedly, it is currently hard to imagine there being sufficient political support on an international scale to negotiate agreements that actually encourage the formation of unions and collective bargaining.

On the other hand, it is not difficult to find broad indications of disgruntlement with current economic policy making. Perhaps those in the antisweatshop and fair trade movements, as well as those unions demonstrating increasing commitment to cross-border collaborations and activism, are building a transnational movement that could eventually mount political support for a more labor-friendly global economy. When combined with other groups disenfranchised by current economic policy making that promotes globalization without taking into consideration the concerns of environmentalists, human rights activists, advocates for the poor, and poor countries themselves, there is a diverse constituency for refocusing the global agenda away from its current course. Such alliances are at the heart of the "social movement unionism" that has been urged as vital to labor's revival (Clawson 2003; Moody 1997; Waterman 1998).

But, as we've also seen throughout this book, not all of the impact of globalization requires a transnational response. Policies shaping and countering the effects of globalization on labor's bargaining power can be made nationally as well. The key is to take steps that ensure the outcomes of expanding economic trade and integration do not undermine labor's bargaining power as a direct economic strategy or an indirect consequence. Indeed, strengthening labor politically, both domestically and internationally, is a symbiotic relationship because national governments have a dual role. They are both actors in their national industrial relations systems and parties to the international agreements that serve as the infrastructure of the global economy. Policymakers shape both the economic changes associated with globalization as well as the manner in which their national industrial relations systems will respond. Therefore, growing labor's political clout in domestic environments could go a long way in strengthening labor protections in international agreements, which would, in turn, further strengthen labor's protections domestically.

For the time being, however, a business agenda dominates economic policy making. At GM, the competitive crisis that forced it into bankruptcy is easing. The company has been restructured, allowed to shed liabilities, and been reborn as a more nimble and profitable automaker. But for GM's workers and autoworkers throughout North America, their turnaround will only come with a return to collective bargaining and respect for workers' rights and working conditions more broadly. Tinkering at the edges to address only the worst labor abuses and sweatshop conditions the global economy has to offer will not alter the more pervasive race to the bottom. While this is a big challenge given labor's weak voice and limited clout, it is otherwise likely that even the best jobs in the global economy will continue to get worse.

Notes

Chapter 1 Introduction

1   While based on actual GM employees, the names of the workers are pseudonyms.
2   The term GM Gypsy was used by workers and managers alike, with no apparent consideration or understanding that it is a derogatory term for the Roma. It has similarly appeared in stories and headlines in widely read newspapers. See, for example: "With Plant Closings, Fewer Jobs for GM Gypsies to Chase," *USA Today*, March 2, 2006; "Where Will 'GM Gypsies' Next Land?" *St. Louis Post Dispatch*, April 4, 2006; "'GM Gypsies' Willing to Keep Moving: If Indiana Site Closes, Workers Can Take Jobs at Plants Elsewhere," *Chicago Tribune*, July 15, 2010.
3   Since 2000, books on sweatshops and possible remedies for them have been published at a rate that exceeds one per year. See, for example, Armbruster-Sandoval 2005; Bender and Greenwald 2003; Bonacich and Appelbaum 2000; Brooks 2007; Collins 2003; Esbenshade 2004; Featherstone 2002; Fung, O'Rourke, and Sabel 2001; Hartman, Arnold, and Wokutch 2003; Louie 2001; Rosen 2002; Ross 2004; Seidman 2007; Sluiter 2009.
4   Both the crisis in U.S. automobile manufacturing and the influx of Japanese transplants have been widely recounted. For a thorough analysis of the establishment of Japanese auto companies and their suppliers in the United States up until the early 1990s, see Kenney and Florida 1993, and especially chapters 4 and 5. For a detailed analysis linking the struggles of the U.S. Big Three automakers, the rise of Japanese transplants, and the overall effects of the coexistence of the two on the geography of auto production in the United States, see Rubenstein 1992.
5   In his plant figures, Rubenstein actually counts assembly lines. So, large plants with more than one assembly line are counted more than once. Furthermore, though a joint project opened in a previously closed plant, he counts the NUMMI auto plant in Fremont, California as a plant closure for GM and an additional foreign-operated plant, perhaps because the agreement between the companies was that Toyota would operate the plant.

Chapter 2 The Intensification of Work under Lean Production

1 As just a partial list, see, for example, Adler 1995, 1999; Adler, Goldoftas, and Levine 1998; Babson 1995b, 1998; Besser 1996; Carrillo 1995; Carrillo and Montiel 1998; Fucini and Fucini 1992; Kochan, Lansbury, and MacDuffie 1997; Liker, Fruin, and Adler 1999; Mishina 1998; Rinehart, Huxley, and Robertson 1997.

Chapter 3 Whipsawed!

1 Details of such incentive packages can be found in local and national newspapers. For examples, see "'Transplant' Car Makers Redefine the Industry," *New York Times*, June 23, 1992; "O Governor, Won't You Buy Me a Mercedes Plant?," *New York Times*, September 1, 1996; "Mississippi Incentives Vie with Alabama for Automaker," *Birmingham News*, September 1, 2000.

Chapter 4 Greenfield Opportunity

1 This figure is skewed by the fact that at the time this research was conducted the plant had only been operating a little over a year, was still hiring, and had a disproportionate share of the workforce at the low end of the pay scale. Upon entering the plant, workers earned a little less than $48 a week. This rose incrementally so that after roughly three months they earn more than $66 a week, with salaries for technicians peaking at $96 a week after eighteen months.

2 All the wage figures are approximations based on the exchange rate at the time of ten pesos to the U.S. dollar.

Chapter 5 Globalization and Union Decline

1 The government's policies were not without dissent from unions, which saw dramatic declines in both their members' standard of livings and their own influence within the government. For a thorough discussion of the mechanisms by which the government exploited rivalries between the major unions to gain widespread concessions, see Murillo 2001.

References

Adler, Paul S. 1995. "'Democratic Taylorism': The Toyota Production System at NUMMI." In *Lean Work: Empowerment and Exploitation in the Global Auto Industry*, edited by Steve Babson, 207–219. Detroit: Wayne State University Press.

———. 1999. "Hybridization: Human Resource Management at Two Toyota Transplants." In *Remade in America: Transplanting and Transforming Japanese Management Systems*, edited by Jeffrey Liker, Mark K. W. Fruin, and Paul S. Adler, 75–116. New York: Oxford University Press.

Adler, Paul S., Barbara Goldoftas, and David I. Levine. 1998. "Stability and Change at NUMMI." In *Between Imitation and Innovation: The Transfer and Hybridization of Productive Models in the International Automobile Industry*, edited by Robert Boyer, Elsie Charron, Ulrich Jurgens, and Steven Tolliday, 128–160. Oxford: Oxford University Press.

Adler, Paul S., Thomas A. Kochan, John Paul MacDuffie, Frits K. Pil, and Saul Rubinstein. 1997. "United States: Variations on a Theme." In *After Lean Production: Evolving Employment Practices in the World Auto Industry*, edited by Thomas Kochan, Russell D. Lansbury, and John Paul MacDuffie, 61–83. Ithaca, NY: Cornell University Press.

Armbruster-Sandoval, Ralph. 2005. *Globalization and Cross-Border Labor Solidarity in the Americas: The Anti-Sweatshop Movement and the Struggle for Social Justice*. New York: Routledge.

Babson, Steve. 1995a. "Lean Production and Labor: Empowerment and Exploitation." In *Lean Work: Empowerment and Exploitation in the Global Auto Industry*, edited by Steve Babson, 1–37. Detroit: Wayne State University Press.

———. 1995b. "Whose Team? Lean Production at Mazda U.S.A." In *Lean Work: Empowerment and Exploitation in the Global Auto Industry*, edited by Steve Babson, 235–246. Detroit: Wayne State University Press.

———. 1998. "Mazda and Ford at Flat Rock: Transfer and Hybridization of the Japanese Model." In *Between Imitation and Innovation: The Transfer and Hybridization of Productive Models in the International Automobile Industry*, edited by Robert Boyer, Elsie Charron, Ulrich Jurgens, and Steven Tolliday, 161–188. New York: Oxford University Press.

———. 2002. "Free Trade and Worker Solidarity in the North American Auto Industry." In *Unions in a Globalized Environment: Changing Borders, Organizational Boundaries, and Social Roles*, edited by Bruce Nissen. Armonk, NY: M. E. Sharpe.

Bair, Jennifer, and Gary Gereffi. 2001. "Local Clusters in Global Chains: The Causes and Consequences of Export Dynamism in Torreon's Blue Jeans Industry." *World Development* 29 (11): 1885–1903.

———. 2003. "Upgrading, Uneven Development, and Jobs in the North American Apparel Industry." *Global Networks* 3 (2):143–169.

Barlett, Donald L., and James Steele. 1998. "States at War." *Time*, November 9.

Barnes, Fred. 2008. "The Other American Auto Industry: Plenty of Car Makers Make a Go of It in This Country—They're Just Non-union and Not Headquartered in Detroit." *Weekly Standard*, December 22.

Barone, Michael. 2008. "Who Is at Fault for the Decline of the Big Three?" *Thomas Jefferson Street blog: U.S. News & World Report*. http://www.usnews.com/opinion/blogs/barone/2008/12/15/who-is-at-fault-for-the-decline-of-the-big-three.

Bayón, Cristina, and Graciela Bensusán. 1998. "Trabajadores y sindicatos ante la globalización: El caso del sector automotriz mexicano." In *Confronting Change: Auto Labor and Lean Production in North America*, edited by Huberto Juarez Núñez and Steve Babson, 117–142. Puebla: Benemérita Universidad Autónoma de Puebla.

Behrens, Martin. 2013. "Germany." In *Comparative Employment Relations in the Global Economy*, edited by Carola Frege and John Kelly, 206–226. London: Routledge.

Bender, Daniel E., and Richard A. Greenwald. 2003. *Sweatshop USA: The American Sweatshop in Historical and Global Perspective*. New York: Routledge.

Bennett, Douglas C., and Kenneth E. Sharpe. 1985. *Transnational Corporations versus the State: The Political Economy of the Mexican Auto Industry*. Princeton: Princeton University Press.

Bensusán, Graciela. 2000. *El modelo mexicano de regulación laboral*. Mexico City: Plaza y Valdés.

———. 2004. "A New Scenario for Mexican Trade Unions: Changes in the Structure of Political and Economic Opportunities." In *Dilemmas of Political Change in Mexico*, edited by Kevin J. Middlebrook. London: Institute of Latin American Studies.

Bensusán, Graciela, and Maria Lorena Cook. 2003. "Political Transition and Labor Revitalization in Mexico." *Research in the Sociology of Work* 11:229–267.

Berggren, Christian. 1992. *Alternatives to Lean Production: Lessons from the Swedish Automobile Industry*. Ithaca, NY: ILR/Cornell University Press.

Besser, Terry L. 1996. *Team Toyota: Transplanting the Toyota Culture to the Camry Plant in Kentucky*, edited by Richard Hall. SUNY Series in the Sociology of Work. Albany: State University of New York Press.

Bonacich, Edna, and Richard Appelbaum. 2000. *Behind the Label: Inequality in the Los Angeles Apparel Industry*. Berkeley: University of California Press.

Boyer, Robert, Elsie Charron, Ulrich Jurgens, and Steven Tolliday, eds. 1998. *Between Imitation and Innovation: The Transfer and Hybridization of Productive Models in the International Automobile Industry*. New York: Oxford University Press.

Braverman, Harry. 1974. *Labor and Monopoly Capital: The Degradation of Work in the Twentieth Century*. New York: Monthley Review Press.

Bronfenbrenner, Kate. 2007. *Global Unions: Challenging Transnational Capital through Cross-Border Campaigns*. Ithaca, NY: Cornell University/ILR Press.

Brooks, Ethel C. 2007. *Unraveling the Garment Industry: Transnational Organizing and Women's Work*, edited by Bert Klandermans. Vol. 27, Social Movements, Protest, and Contention. Minneapolis: University of Minnesota Press.

Brown, Kevin C. 2011. "A Tale of Two Systems." *Remapping Debate: Asking "Why" and "Why Not"* website, New York. http://www.remappingdebate.org/article/tale-two -systems.

Bueno, Carmen. 1998. "De la produccion nacional a la competencia global: El caso de la industria mexicana de autopartes." In *Confronting Change: Auto Labor, and Lean Production in North America*, edited by Huberto Juarez Núñez and Steve Babson, 281–302. Puebla: Benemérita Universidad Autónoma de Puebla.

Burawoy, Michael. 1979. *Manufacturing Consent: Changes in the Labor Process under Monopoly Capitalism*. Chicago: University of Chicago Press.

———. 1985. *The Politics of Production: Factory Regimes under Capitalism and Socialism*. London: Verso.

———. 1998. "The Extended Case Method." *Sociological Theory* 16 (1): 4–33.

———. 2009. *The Extended Case Method: Four Countries, Four Decades, Four Great Transformations, and One Theoretical Tradition*. Berkeley: University of California Press.

Burns, Joe. 2011. *Reviving the Strike: How Working People Can Regain Power and Transform America*. Brooklyn, NY: IG Publishing.

Cappelli, P., and D. Neumark. 2001. "Do 'High-Performance' Work Practices Improve Establishment Level Outcomes?" *Industrial and Labor Relations Review* no. 54:737–776.

Carrillo, Jorge. 1995. "Flexible Production in the Auto Sector: Industrial Reorganization at Ford-Mexico." *World Development* 23 (1): 87–101.

Carrillo, Jorge, and Hualde Alfredo. 1998. "Maquiladoras en redes: El caso de Delphi-GM." In *Confronting Change: Auto Labor and Lean Production in North America*, edited by Huberto Juarez Núñez and Steve Babson, 369–385. Puebla: Benemérita Universidad Autónoma de Puebla.

Carrillo, Jorge, and Yolanda Montiel. 1998. "Ford's Hermosillo Plant: The Trajectory of Development of a Hybrid Model." In *Between Imitation and Innovation: The Transfer and Hybridization of Productive Models in the International Automobile Industry*, edited by Robert Boyer, Elsie Charron, Ulrich Jurgens, and Steven Tolliday, 295–318. New York: Oxford University Press.

Caulfield, Norman. 2004. "Labor Relations in Mexico: Historical Legacies and Some Recent Trends." *Labor History* 45 (4): 445–467.

Center for Automotive Research. 2005. *The Contribution of the International Auto Sector to the U.S. Economy: An Update*. Ann Arbor: Center for Automotive Research.

Clawson, Dan. 2003. *The Next Upsurge: Labor and the New Social Movements*. Ithaca, NY: Cornell University Press.

Clawson, Dan, and Mary Ann Clawson. 1999. "What Has Happened to the U.S. Labor Movement? Union Decline and Renewal." *Annual Review of Sociology* no. 25:95–119.

Collier, Ruth B., and David Collier. 1991. *Shaping the Political Arena: Critical Junctures, the Labor Movement, and Regime Dynamics in Latin America*. Princeton: Princeton University Press.

Collins, Jane L. 2003. *Threads: Gender, Labor, and Power in the Global Apparel Industry*. Chicago: University of Chicago Press.

Compa, Lance. 1995. "The First NAFTA Labor Cases: A New International Labor Rights Regime Takes Shape." *U.S.-Mexico Law Journal* no. 3: 159–181.

Cornette, Guy. 1999. "Saturn: Re-engineering the New Industrial Relations." In *Teamwork in the Automobile Industry: Radical Change or Passing Fashion?*, edited by Jean-Pierre Durand, Paul Stewart, and Juan José Castillo, 85–106. London: Macmillan Press.

Crowley, Martha, Daniel Tope, Lindsey Joyce Chamberlain, and Randy Hodson. 2010. "Neo-Taylorism at Work: Occupational Change in the Post-Fordist Era." *Social Problems* 57 (3): 421–447.

Dassbach, Carl H. A. 1996. "Lean Production, Labor Control, and Post-Fordism in the Japanese Automobile Industry." In *North American Auto Unions in Crisis*, edited by William C. Green and Ernest J. Yanarella, 19–40. Albany: State University of New York Press.

de la Garza, Enrique. 1994. "The Restructuring of State-Labor Relations in Mexico." In *The Politics of Economic Restructuring: State-Society Relations and Regime Change in Mexico*, edited by Lorena Maria Cook, Kevin J. Middlebrook, and J. M. Horcasitas, 195–217. San Diego: Center for U.S.-Mexican Studies.

———. 1998. "Modelos de producción, estratégias empresariales y relaciones laborales." In *Estrategias de modernización empresarial en México, flexibilidad y control sobre el proceso de trabajo*, edited by Enrique de la Garza, 243–261. Mexico City: Rayuela Editores.

Doh, Jonathan P. 1998. "The Impact of NAFTA on the Auto Industry in the United States." In *The North American Auto Industry under NAFTA*, edited by Sidney Weintraub and Christopher Sands, 15–47. Washington, DC: Center for Strategic and International Studies.

Dohse, Knuth, Ulrich Jurgens, and Thomas Nialsch. 1985. "From 'Fordism' to 'Toyotism'? The Social Organization of the Labor Process in the Japanese Automobile Industry." *Politics & Society* 14 (2): 115–146.

Due, Jesper, Jorgen Steen Madsen, and Carsten Stroby Jensen. 1991. "The Social Dimension: Convergence or Diversification of IR in the Single European Market?" *Industrial Relations Journal* 22 (2): 85–102.

Dunlop, John. 1958. *Industrial Relations Systems*. New York: Holt.

Durand, Jean-Pierre, Paul Stewart, and Juan Jose Castillo. 1999a. "Conclusion: The Transformation of Employee Relations in the Automobile Industry?" In *Teamwork in the Automobile Industry: Radical Change or Passing Fashion?*, edited by Jean-Pierre Durand, Paul Stewart, and Juan Jose Castillo, 412–445. London: Macmillan Press.

———, eds. 1999b. *Teamwork in the Automobile Industry: Radical Change or Passing Fashion?* London: Macmillan Press.

Esbenshade, Jill. 2004. *Monitoring Sweatshops: Workers, Consumers, and the Global Apparel Industry*. Philadelphia: Temple University Press.

Evans, Peter. 2008. "Is an Alternative Globalization Possible?" *Politics & Society* 36 (2): 271–305.

Farris, David, and Edward Levine. 2004. "Declining Union Density in Mexico, 1984–2000." *Monthly Labor Review* 127 (9): 10–16.

Featherstone, Liza. 2002. *Students against Sweatshops: The Making of a Movement*. New York: Verso.

Friedman, Thomas L. 2005. *The World Is Flat: A Brief History of the Twenty-First Century*. New York: Farrar, Straus and Giroux.

Fucini, Joseph J., and Suzy Fucini. 1992. *Working for the Japanese: Inside Mazda's American Auto Plant*. New York: Free Press.

Fujimoto, Takahiro. 1999. *The Evolution of a Manufacturing System at Toyota*. New York: Oxford University Press.

Fung, Archon, Dara O'Rourke, and Charles Sabel. 2001. *Can We Put an End to Sweatshops?* Boston: Beacon Press.

García, A., and A. Lara. 1998. "Cambio tecnológico y aprendizaje laboral en G.M.: Los casos del D.F. y Silao." In *Confronting Change: Auto Labor and Lean Production in North America*, edited by Huberto Núñez and Steve Babson, 207–222. Puebla: Benemérita Universidad Autónoma de Puebla.

Garcia, P. Roberto, and Stephen Hills. 1998. "Meeting Lean Competitors: Ford de México's Industrial Relations Strategy." In *Confronting Change: Auto Labor and Lean Production in North America*, edited by Huberto Juarez Núñez and Steve Babson, 143–154. Puebla: Benemérita Universidad Autónoma de Puebla.

Gereffi, Gary. 1994. "The Organization of Buyer-Driven Global Commodity Chains: How U.S. Retailers Shape Overseas Production Networks." In *Commodity Chains and Global Capitalism*, edited by Gary Gereffi, Miguel Korzeniewicz, and Roberto P. Korzeniewicz, 95–122. Westport, CT: Praeger Publishers.

———. 1999. "International Trade and Industrial Upgrading in the Apparel Commodity Chain." *Journal of International Economics* no. 40:37–70.

Gereffi, Gary, John Humphrey, Raphael Kaplinsky, and Timothy J. Sturgeon. 2001. "Introduction: Globalisation, Value Chains, and Development." In *The Value of Value Chains: Spreading the Gains from Globalisation*, edited by Gary Gereffi and Raphael Kaplinsky. Special issue, *IDS Bulletin* 32, no. 3 (July): 1–8. Brighton, UK: Institute of Development Studies, University of Sussex.

Godard, John. 2004. "A Critical Assessment of the High-Performance Paradigm." *British Journal of Industrial Relations* 42 (2): 349–378.

Goldfield, Michael. 1989. *The Decline of Organized Labor in the United States.* Chicago: University of Chicago Press.

Gordon, Michael E., and Lowell Turner. 2000. *Transnational Cooperation among Labor Unions.* Ithaca, NY: Cornell University/ILR Press.

Gould, William B. 2013. *A Primer on American Labor Law.* Vol. 5. Cambridge: Cambridge University Press.

Graham, Laurie. 1995. *On the Line at Subaru-Isuzu: The Japanese Model and the American Worker.* Ithaca, NY: Cornell University Press.

Grayson, G. 1989. *The Mexican Labor Machine: Power, Politics, and Patronage.* Washington, DC: Center for Strategic and International Studies.

Greer, Charles R., Charles D. Stevens, and Gregory K. Stephens. 2007. "The State of the Unions in Mexico." *Journal of Labor Research* 28 (1): 69–92.

The Harbour Report North America. 1999–2005. Troy, MI: Harbour and Associates.

Harrison, Bennett. 1994. *Lean and Mean: The Changing Landscape of Corporate Power in the Age of Flexibility.* New York: Basic Books.

Hartman, Laura P., Denis Arnold, and Richard A. Wokutch. 2003. *Rising above Sweatshops: Innovative Approaches to Global Labor Challenges.* Westport, CT: Praeger.

Helper, Susan. 1995. *Supplier Relations and Adoption of New Technology: Results of Survey Research in the U.S. Auto Industry.* National Bureau of Economic Research Working Paper. Cambridge, MA: NBER.

Helper, Susan, John Paul MacDuffie, and Charles Sabel. 2000. "Pragmatic Collaborations: Advancing Knowledge While Controlling Opportunism." *Industrial and Corporate Change* 9 (3): 443–488.

Holmes, John. 1993. "From Three Industries to One: Toward an Integrated North American Automobile Industry." In *Driving Continentally: National Policies and the North*

American Auto Industry, edited by Maureen Appel Molot, 23–62. Ottawa: Carleton University Press.

Humphrey, John. 2000. "Assembler-Supplier Relations in the Auto Industry: Globalization and National Development." *Competition & Change* no. 4:245–271.

Humphrey, John, and Olga Memedovic. 2003. *The Global Automotive Industry Value Chain: What Prospects for Upgrading by Developing Countries.* Vienna: United Nations Industrial Development Organization.

Ichniowski, Casey, Kathryn Shaw, and Giovanna Prennushi. 1997. "The Effects of Human Resource Management Practices on Productivity: A Study of Steel Finishing Lines." *American Economic Review* 87 (3): 291–314.

Kalleberg, Arne L. 2011. *Good Jobs, Bad Jobs: The Rise of Polarized and Precarious Employment Systems in the United States, 1970s–2000s.* American Sociological Association's Rose Series in Sociology. New York: Russell Sage Foundation.

Kaminska, Monika Ewa. 2013. "Regional Regulation: The EU and NAFTA." In *Comparative Employment Relations in the Global Economy*, edited by Carola Frege and John Kelly, 407–424. London: Routledge.

Katz, Harry C. 1985. *Shifting Gears: Changing Labor Relations in the U.S. Automobile Industry.* Cambridge, MA: MIT Press.

Katz, Harry C., and Owen Darbishire. 2000. *Converging Divergencies: Worldwide Changes in Employment Systems.* Ithaca, NY: Cornell/ILR Press.

Katz, Harry C., John Paul MacDuffie, and Frits K. Pil. 2002. "Collective Bargaining in the U.S. Auto Industry." In *Collective Bargaining in the Private Sector*, edited by Paul F. Clark, John T. Delaney, and Ann C. Frost. Champaign, IL: Industrial Relations Research Association.

———. 2013. "Crisis and Recovery in the U.S. Auto Industry: Tumultuous Times for a Collective Bargaining Pacesetter." In *Collective Bargaining under Duress: Case Studies of Major North American Industries*, edited by Howard R. Stranger, Paul F. Clark, and Ann C. Frost. Champaign, IL: Labor and Employment Relations Association.

Kay, Tamara. 2005. "Labor Transnationalism and Global Governance: The Impact of NAFTA on Transnational Labor Relationships in North America." *American Journal of Sociology* 111 (3): 715–756.

Kenney, Martin, and Richard Florida. 1993. *Beyond Mass Production: The Japanese System and Its Transfer to the U.S.* New York: Oxford University Press.

———. 1994. "Japanese Maquiladoras: Production Organization and Global Commodity Chains." *World Development* 22 (1): 27–44.

Kochan, Thomas A. 2001. "Can the U.S. Industrial Relations System be Transformed? The Role of Ideas, Reform Efforts, and Social Crisis." In *Sourcebook of Labor Markets: Evolving Structures and Processes*, edited by Ivar Berg and Arne Kalleberg, 83–100. New York: Plenum Publishers.

Kochan, Thomas A., Harry C. Katz, and Robert B. McKersie. 1994. *The Transformation of American Industrial Relations.* Ithaca, NY: Cornell University/ILR Press.

Kochan, Thomas A., Russel D. Lansbury, and John Paul MacDuffie, eds. 1997. *After Lean Production: Evolving Employment Practices in the World Auto Industry.* Ithaca, NY: Cornell University Press.

Krzywdzinski, Martin. 2014. "Do Investors Avoid Strong Trade Unions and Labour Regulation? Social Dumping in the European Automotive and Chemical Industries." *Work, Employment & Society* 28 (6): 926–945.

Kumar, Pradeep, and John Holmes. 1998. "The Impact of NAFTA on the Auto Industry in Canada." In *The North American Auto Industry under NAFTA*, edited by Sidney Weintraub and Christopher Sands, 92–183. Washington, DC: Center for Strategic and International Studies.

Kwon, Hyeong-Ki. 2003. "Divergent Constitution of Liberal Regimes: Comparison of the U.S. and German Automotive Supplier Markets." *Politics & Society* 31 (1): 93–130.

La Botz, Dan. 1992. *Mask of Democracy*. Boston: South End Press.

———. 2005. "Mexico's Labor Movement in Transition." *Monthly Review* 57 (2): 62–72. http://monthlyreview.org/2005/06/01/mexicos-labor-movement-in-transition/.

Lee, Ching Kwan. 2007. *Against the Law: Labor Protests in China's Rustbelt and Sunbelt*. Berkeley: University of California Press.

Levine, David I., and Laura D'Andrea Tyson. 1990. "Participation, Productivity, and the Firm's Environment." In *Paying for Productivity: A Look at the Evidence*, edited by Alan S. Blinder. Washington, DC: Brookings Institution.

Lichtenstein, Nelson. 1992. "Reutherism on the Shop Floor: Union Strategy and Shop Floor Conflict in the USA 1946–70." In *Between Fordism and Flexibility: The Automobile Industry and Its Workers*, edited by Steven Tolliday and Jonathan Zeitlin, 121–143. Oxford: Berg Publishers.

Liker, Jeffrey K., Mark W. Fruin, and Paul S. Adler. 1999. *Remade in America: Transplanting and Transforming Japanese Management Systems*. New York: Oxford University Press.

Louie, Miriam Ching Yoon. 2001. *Sweatshop Warriors: Immigrant Women Workers Take On the Global Factory*. Cambridge, MA: South End Press.

MacDuffie, John Paul, and Frits K. Pil. 1997. "Changes in Auto Industry Employment Practices: An International Overview." In *After Lean Production: Evolving Employment Practices in the World Auto Industry*, edited by Thomas A. Kochan, Russell D. Lansbury, and John Paul MacDuffie, 9–42. Ithaca: Cornell University Press.

Martin, Christopher R. 2004. *Framed! Labor and the Corporate Media*. Ithaca, NY: Cornell University/ILR Press.

Maynard, Micheline, and Michael J. de la Merced. 2009. "G.M. Pushes the Case for Its Rebirth in Court." *New York Times*, June 30, B6.

McMichael, Philip. 2008. *Development and Social Change: A Global Perspective*. 4th ed. Thousand Oaks, CA: Pine Forge Press.

Micheli, Jordy. 1994. *Nueva manufactura globalización y producción de automóviles en México*. Mexico City: Universidad Nacional Autónoma de México.

Middlebrook, Kevin J. 1989. "Union Democratization in the Mexican Automobile Industry: A Reappraisal." *Latin American Research Review* 24 (2): 69–94.

———. 1995. *The Paradox of Revolution: Labor, the State, and Authoritarianism in Mexico*. Baltimore: Johns Hopkins University Press.

Milkman, Ruth. 1997. *Farewell to the Factory: Auto Workers in the Late Twentieth Century*. Berkeley: University of California Press.

Mishina, K. 1998. "Making Toyota in America: Evidence from the Kentucky Transplant, 1986–1994." In *Between Imitation and Innovation: The Transfer and Hybridization of Productive Models in the International Automobile Industry*, edited by Robert Boyer, Elsie Charron, Ulrich Jurgens, and Steven Tolliday, 99–127. New York: Oxford University Press.

Moody, Kim. 1997. *Workers in a Lean World: Unions in the International Economy*, edited by Mike Davis and Michael Sprinker. Haymarket Series. New York: Verso.

Murillo, M. V. 2001. "Partisan Loyalty and Union Competition: Macroeconomic Adjustment and Industrial Restructuring in Mexico." In *The Politics of Labor in a Global Age: Continuity and Change in Late-Industrializing and Post-Socialist Economies*, edited by C. Candland and R. Sil, 31–68. New York: Oxford University Press.

Nissen, Bruce. 2003. "The Recent Past and Near Future of Private Sector Unionism in the U.S.: An Appraisal." *Journal of Labor Research* 24 (2): 323–338.

Osterman, Paul, and Beth Shulman. 2011. *Good Jobs America: Making Work Better for Everyone*. New York: Russell Sage Foundation.

Parker, Mike. 1993. "Industrial Relations Myth and Shop Floor Reality: The 'Team Concept' in the Auto Industry." In *Industrial Democracy in America: The Ambiguous Promise*, edited by Nelson Lichtenstein and Howell John Harris, 249–274. Cambridge: Cambridge University Press.

Parker, Mike, and Jane Slaughter. 1995. "Unions and Management by Stress." In *Lean Work: Empowerment and Exploitation in the Global Auto Industry*, edited by Steve Babson, 41–53. Detroit: Wayne State University Press.

Plankey-Videla, Nancy. 2012. *We Are in This Dance Together: Gender, Power, and Globalization at a Mexican Garment Firm*. New Brunswick, NJ: Rutgers University Press.

Pries, Ludger. 2000. *Entre el corporativismo productivista y la participación de los trabajadores: Globalización y relaciones industriales en la industria automotriz Mexicana*. Mexico City: Miguel Ángel Porrúa.

Ramirez de la O, R. 1998. "The Impact of NAFTA on the Auto Industry in Mexico." In *The North American Auto Industry under NAFTA*, edited by Sidney Weintraub and Christopher Sands, 48–91. Washington, DC: Center for Strategic and International Studies.

Rinehart, James, Christopher Huxley, and David Robertson. 1997. *Just Another Car Factory? Lean Production and Its Discontents*. Ithaca, NY: Cornell University Press.

Rosen, Ellen Israel. 2002. *Making Sweatshops: The Globalization of the U.S. Apparel Industry*. Berkeley: University of California Press.

Rosenfeld, Jake. 2014. *What Unions No Longer Do*. Cambridge, MA: Harvard University Press.

Ross, Robert J. S. 2004. *Slaves to Fashion: Poverty and Abuse in the New Sweatshops*. Ann Arbor: University of Michigan Press.

Rothstein, Jeffrey S. 2004. "Creating Lean Industrial Relations: General Motors in Silao, Mexico." *Competition & Change* 8 (3): 203–222.

———. 2005. "Economic Development Policymaking Down the Global Commodity Chain: Attracting an Auto Industry to Silao, Mexico." *Social Forces* 84 (1): 49–69.

———. 2006. "The Uncertain Future of the American Auto Industry." *New Labor Forum* 15 (2): 65–73.

———. 2008. "Lean Times: UAW Concessions in the New Auto Industry Labor Agreement." *New Labor Forum* 17 (2): 61–69.

Roxborough, Ian. 1984. *Unions and Politics in Mexico: The Case of the Automobile Industry*. Cambridge: Cambridge University Press.

Rubenstein, James M. 1992. *The Changing U.S. Auto Industry: A Geographical Analysis*. New York: Routledge.

Rubinstein, Saul, and Thomas Kochan. 2001. *Learning from Saturn: Possibilities for Corporate Governance and Employee Relations*. Ithaca, NY: ILR Press.

Ruckelshaus, Catherine, and Sarah Leberstein. 2014. *Manufacturing Low Pay: Declining Wages in the Jobs That Built America's Middle Class*. New York: National Employment Law Project.

Salzinger, Leslie. 2003. *Genders in Production: Making Workers in Mexico's Global Factories.* Berkeley: University of California Press.

Sanchez, Miguel Angel Ramirez. 2011. "Los sindicatos blancos de Monterrey (1931–2009)." *Frontera Norte* 23 (46): 177–210.

Sassen, Saskia. 2007. *A Sociology of Globalization.* Edited by Jeffrey C. Alexander. Contemporary Societies. New York: W. W. Norton.

Schaeffer, Robert K. 2009. *Understanding Globalization: The Social Consequences of Political, Economic, and Environmental Change.* 4th ed. Lanham, MD: Rowman & Littlefield.

Seidman, Gay W. 2007. *Beyond the Boycott: Labor Rights, Human Rights, and Transnational Activism.* Rose Series in Sociology. New York: Russell Sage Foundation.

Shaiken, Harley. 1990. *Mexico in the Global Economy: High Technology and Work Organization in Export Industries.* Center for U.S.-Mexican Studies Monograph Series. San Diego: UC San Diego, Center for U.S.-Mexican Studies.

———. 1994. "Advanced Manufacturing and Mexico: A New International Division of Labor?" *Latin American Research Review* 29 (2): 39–71.

Shaiken, Harley, Steven Lopez, and Isaac Mankita. 1997. "Two Routes to Team Production: Saturn and Chrysler Compared." *Industrial Relations* 36 (1): 17–45.

Silver, Beverly J. 2003. *Forces of Labor: Workers' Movements and Globalization since 1870.* Cambridge Studies in Comparative Politics. New York: Cambridge University Press.

Sluiter, Liesbeth. 2009. *Clean Clothes: A Global Movement to End Sweatshops.* London: Pluto Press.

Soden, Dennis L., Fred Cady, Rogelio Carrasco, Matthew McElroy, and Lorena Orozco. 2001. *The Delphi Decision: A Case Study.* El Paso: University of Texas at El Paso Public Policy Research Center.

Taylor, Frederick Winslow. 1911. *Principles of Scientific Management.* New York: Harper & Brothers.

Tolliday, Steven, and Jonathan Zeitlin. 1992. "Shop-Floor Bargaining, Contract Unionism, and Job Control: An Anglo-American Comparison." In *Between Fordism and Flexibility: The Automobile Industry and Its Workers*, edited by Steven Tolliday and Jonathan Zeitlin, 99–120. Oxford: Berg Publishers.

Tsutsui, William M. 1998. *Manufacturing Ideology: Scientific Management in Twentieth-Century Japan.* Princeton: Princeton University Press.

Tuman, John P. 1998. "The Political Economy of Restructuring in Mexico's 'Brownfield' Plants: A Comparative Analysis." In *Transforming the Latin American Automobile Industry: Unions, Workers, and the Politics of Restructuring*, edited by John P. Tuman and John T. Morris, 148–178. Armonk, NY: M. E. Sharpe.

UAW Local 95. *UAW 50 Years.* 1985. Written and edited by Howard A. Milbrandt, Richard Costerisan, and John O Meara. Beloit, WI: Vance Printing.

U.S. Bureau of Labor Statistics. 2014. *Union Members Summary.* Washington, DC.

U.S. Senate. 2008. Committee on Banking, Housing, and Urban Affairs. *Testimony of Ron Gettelfinger, President, International Union, United Automobile, Aerospace & Agricultural Implement Workers of America (UAW) on the Subject of Examining the State of the Domestic Automobile Industry.* November 18.

Vallas, Steven P. 1999. "Rethinking Post-Fordism: The Meanings of Workplace Flexibility." *Sociological Theory* no. 17:68–101.

———. 2006. "Empowerment Redux: Structure, Agency, and the Remaking of Managerial Authority." *American Journal of Sociology* 111 (6): 1677–1717.

Veloso, F. 2000. *The Automotive Supply Chain Organization: Global Trends and Perspectives.* Massachusetts Institute of Technology Working Paper. Cambridge, MA: MIT.

Vidal, Matt. 2007. "Lean Production, Worker Empowerment, and Job Satisfaction: A Qualitative Analysis and Critique." *Critical Sociology* no. 33:247–278.

von Bülow, M. 1998. "Restructuración productiva y estrategias sindicales: El caso de Ford-Cuautitlán (1987–1994)." In *Flexibles y Productivos? Estudios Sobre Flexibilidad Laboral en Mexico*, edited by Francisco Zapata, 143–173. Mexico City: El Colegio de México.

Waterman, Peter. 1998. *Globalization, Social Movements, and the New Internationalisms.* Employment and Work Relations in Context Series. Washington, DC: Mansell Publishing.

Webster, Edward, Robert Lambert, and Andries Bezuidenhout. 2008. *Grounding Globalization: Labour in the Age of Insecurity.* Malden, MA: Blackwell Publishing.

Womack, James P., Daniel T. Jones, and Daniel Roos. 1990. *The Machine That Changed the World.* New York: Rawson Associates.

Index

Page numbers in italics refer to figures; numbers followed by T designate tables.

intellectual engagement, workers', under GMS, 34, 38, 62, 65
intensification of work, 66, 148; under GMS, 34, 36, 39, 58 (*see also* speedups)
International Monetary Fund, 139
International Union, Automobile, Aerospace and Agricultural Implement Workers of America, *see* United Auto Workers
"inverse layoff," 47
ISI (import substitution industrialization), in Mexico, 19, 132–134, 139, 150

Janesville GM plant, 2–3, 25, 28; abandonment of "jointness" in, 89–90, 97; age of, 5; Andon system, 41T, 51–54, 95; Chevrolet division, 70, 72; concession bargaining at, 29, 30; Depression era through 1960s, 71; employee participation/input in, 35, 40, 58–60, 69–70, 94; Fisher Body division, 70, 74; globalization as doom at, 8–12; implementation of Core Requirements Tracking System at, 36–37; intensification of work, under GMS, 38, 39; "jointness" experiment, 80–83; last days and closing of, 94–95; productivity at, 64; and recession-driven cutbacks, 77–78; seniority system, 10–11, 44–45, 46; SUV production ramped up, 92, 93; teamwork in, 34, 35, 44–47, 69–70, 94; unionizes, 72; whipsawing of, 29, 69, 97, 98
Japanese automakers: management style, 33; and transplant factories, 22–23, 144. *See also individual companies*
J. D. Power, 67
job classifications: consolidation of, 25, 75, 79, 84; of mass-production era, 74
job creation, in non-GM-related Silao firms, 104–105
job descriptions, 69
job quality, decline in, 62, 66, 81, 144, 155. *See also* intensification of work; speedups
job rotation, 40, 42, 48, 66; opposition to, in Janesville, 45
jobs banks, 47, 136
"jointness" program, Janesville, 80–83, 88; abandonment of, 89–94, 97
just-in-time delivery, 35–36, 71, 100, 104, 119

kaizen, 32, 56, 57, 62, 66
Katz, Harry, 128
Korean transplant factories, 144; Kia and Hyundai, 23

labor: activist/militant, 4, 133, 148–149, 153; blacklisted "poor quality workers," 117; of children, 152, 156; declining bargaining power of, 29–30, 124, 149–150; employee buyouts, 138; "empowered" through participation/input, 36, 81 (*see also* participation); forced, prohibition of, 152, 156; in the global economy, 14–15, 25–27, 70, 148–149; intellectual engagement of, 32, 34, 62; migrant worker protections, under NAALC, 153; nonunion, in auto industry, 148, 150; right to organize, 152, 154, 156; shop floor flexibility, 25; temporary workers, in Mexico, 133; turnover, 99, 108–109, 111–112, 114, 117, 118; of women (*see* women workers)
Labor and Employment Relations Association, 125
labor contracts, local, 69, 74; function redefined by management, 84
labor law: European Union, 151–152; Mexican, 130–134; U.S., and "right-to-work" laws, 126–127, 137
labor-management cooperation, concession bargaining as, 76, 81
labor relations: coordinated, at Silao plant, 116–120; at Janesville plant, 72–75; during Mexico's implementation of ISI, 132–134; under "treaty of Detroit," 128–129
labor standards, international, 155–157
Lagermex, 104
layoffs, 46–47, 76, 77, 129
lean production, 18, 20, 28, 31–34, 88; compared with GMS, 35–37; and disregard of systemic problems, 53; in European Union, 151; and globalization, 24–25; and just-in-time component contractors, 100; and labor relations, in Silao, 117; *vs.* mass production, 64–65, 70; and standardized work, 61–64; at transplant factories, as model, 136, 148; willingness of workforce to implement, 68. *See also* Global Manufacturing System

OCP (Occupational Change Process), 37
"official" unions, Mexican, 131, 140, 141, 148
oil crisis, post-1979, 77
Oldsmobile 88, 84
overtime, 2, 12
Oxford Automotriz, 102T, 104, 105, 117

PAN (National Action Party), Mexico, 143
participation, employee, 35, 36; in Arlington,
    41T, 70; consultative system, 56; in Janes-
    ville, 35, 40, 41T, 69–70, 94; logic of, 54;
    in Silao, 41T. *See also* input
parts shortages, 64
parts suppliers, 24, 100
pattern bargaining, 128; demise of, 135–137
pay hierarchy: *vs.* "equal pay for equal work"
    principle, 138; in Silao plants, 117–118, 122,
    164n.1 (ch.4). *See also* wages
PEMEX, 118
pensions, 129
Perot, H. Ross, 155
peso: devaluations of, 21, 139, 142; exchange
    rate with dollar, 164n.2
pickup trucks, *see* trucks
plant closings, 23
"Points of the Star" system, Silao, 43
Pontiac, Michigan, GM plant, 84, 91
Pontiac brand: Chieftain, 72; end of produc-
    tion, 147
"poor quality workers," 117
"post-Fordist" approach, in analysis of lean
    production, 32
PRI (Institutional Revolutionary Party,
    Mexico), 130, 133; loses to National
    Action Party, 143; new economic policies
    of 1980s, 139; ties to "official" unions, 141,
    150
product demand, 5, 93
production: elimination of defects in, 65;
    footprint (*see* footprint); growth of, in
    mass production era, 70
productivity, 84, 88, 96; decline, spikes in,
    and new vehicle launches, 64; HPV as
    measure of, 62–64, *63*; increases, in Mex-
    ico, and real wage loss, 142; made focus
    of Janesville plant, 89, 94; unaffected by
    substantive worker participation, 36; of
    union *vs.* non-union auto workers, 67

protection contracts, 140
Puebla, Mexico, Volkswagen plant, 132

quality: of product, 52–53, 62, 84; of work-
    ing conditions, decline in, 81, 144, 155 (*see
    also* intellectual engagement; working
    conditions)
quality engineers, 51
"Quality Network," GM, 82
"Quality of Work Life" programs, 81–82
quotas, of Japanese autos exported to U.S., 22

"race to the bottom," 149, 151, 162
Ramos Arizpe, GM plant, 111
recessions: Great, post-2008, 31; post-1979,
    77; post-Vietnam, 76
recruitment, at Silao GM plant, 114–116
Renault, 19
repetitive motion, 40; injuries from, 10
retirement packages: employee buyouts, 138;
    at transplants, 135–136
Reuther, Walter, 128
Richards, Ann, 86
right to organize, 152, 154, 156
"right-to-work" laws, 126–127, 137
robots, 77
rotation among jobs, 40, 42, 48, 66; opposi-
    tion to, in Janesville, 45
Rubenstein, James M., 23, 163n.53

Saab, 147
safety and health: ergonomic challenges, in
    standardized work routines, 40; Euro-
    pean Union standards, 151; injury preven-
    tion and treatment, under NAALC, 153;
    in local contract negotiations, 70; repeti-
    tive motion injuries, 10
Salinas de Gortari, Carlos, 101
Samson Tractors, 8–9, 70
San Antonio, Texas, Toyota plant, 136
Saturn, 36, 147
section committees, Mexican, 108
Section Four, SITIMM, 109–114
Seglo, 102T, 104, 118
seniority systems, 69; at Arlington, 13, 48; in
    Janesville, 10–11, 44–45, 46, 93, 95; and
    UAW's 2007 contract, 138; weakened, in
    lean production, 25

About the Author

JEFFREY ROTHSTEIN is an associate professor of sociology at Grand Valley State University near Grand Rapids, Michigan. He teaches and writes about the changing nature of work in the global economy and the impact of globalization on labor in the United States and abroad. His work has appeared in a number of journals, including *Social Forces, Competition & Change, Research in the Sociology of Work, Critical Sociology*, and *New Labor Forum*.

CPSIA information can be obtained
at www.ICGtesting.com
Printed in the USA
LVOW11s0202020617

536663LV00001B/93/P